SPEAKING OF FREEDOM

Collected Poems

ALYN HASKEY

W0013841

FREEDOM MINISTRIES

in association with

MOORLEY'S Print & Publishing

© Copyright 1997 Alyn Haskey

All rights reserved. No part of this publication may be
reproduced, stored in a retrieval system, or
transmitted, in any form or by any means,
electronic, mechanical, photocopying, recording
or otherwise, without the prior
written permission of the publishers.

British Library Cataloguing in Publication Data.
A catalogue record for this book is available
from the British Library.

MOORLEY'S Print & Publishing
23 Park Rd., Ilkeston, Derbys DE7 5DA
Tel/Fax: (0115) 932 0643

ISBN 0 86071 489 6

FOREWORD

Poetry, at its best, should be precise, restless and comforting. Poetry should have many moods; it should pray, but also proclaim, coming at us, to quote much missed Orkney Poet, George Mackay Brown, in 'a gale of psalms'. Poetry should lament, protest, yet converse with chiselled speech, but most of all poetry should be the 'unraised' voice in the blaring babble of the world.

Alyn Haskey's poetic voice and speech flows with thoughtful observation, warmth and delicacy. His poetry carries an authority of experience and insight which we in the striding world need to hear for the sake of our our own paralysed spirits.

The Victorian hymn writer, Horatius Bonar, implored his hearers 'to take up the torch and wave it wide'. In his poetry and his life Alyn Haskey goes about such a task. His work seeps into you. Allow it to. We all so need it.

Stewart Henderson
Scotland
January 1997

Chapter 1
Verse for Everyone (1975)

Alyn says: It was a time of new experiences, going to Buckingham Palace to receive my Duke of Edinburgh Gold Award, gaining a place at university and getting used to the rigours of study. It was also a time of being famous, being given the Spastics Society Achievement Award.

Foreword

In our first magazine we cover the work of Alyn Haskey who started us out on this venture.

AN INSPIRATION TO ALL

Alyn Haskey is 23 years old, a spastic who, despite terrible handicaps, made it to prestigious University of York, where he is studying History and Sociology. On March 3rd this year he won The Spastic Society's Achievement of the Year Award, for which he received a cheque for £250, plus a medal and a silver cup.

Alyn, who is in a wheel chair, has poor speech and cannot feed or dress himself. His only method of writing is by operating an electric typewriter by a stick held between his teeth.

However, he aims to finish his University course in the normal three years, despite his handicap.

From eleven to sixteen years of age Alyn was in a school for the educationally sub-normal children, but his achievements since those days are very impressive. He has won the Duke of Edinburgh's Bronze, Silver and Gold Awards, written plays, songs, poems and serial stories. When not studying Alyn paints, holding a brush between his teeth and he is Sports Writer for York University. He has won numerous prizes in the games and sports for the disabled.

Alyn is looked after by a member of the Community Service Volunteers who has a room next to his at Alcuin College.

IMAGINATION

In my time machine
I am free.
No longer strapped in a wheel chair
But able to drift,
Drift,
Drift.

Through the corridors of time,
Across the barriers of space,
To see things that have never been seen before,
Moving towards happiness,
Coming to a brand new universe
Where I am free.

* * *

MIRACLES

Do you believe in Miracles?
Or in some magic plan?
Do you believe that things work out?
If you do, then they can.
There's a man who lives on high
Who can do just anything,
His ways, they are mysterious
His methods, they are sure,
Be ready for the call
It may be your next chore.
He brings us all together
He gives us peace and love,
So, let us join together
In fellowship from above.

WAR SHOULD BE ENDED

Millions die,
Flames leap high,
People cry,
Politicians sigh -
War should be ended

Death walks,
Fear stalks,
Guns talk,
Houses crumble like chalk -
War should be ended.

Count the cost.
People lost,
Humanity tossed,
Soldiers bossed -
War should be ended.

Survivors moan,
Living alone,
Lost all they own,
Seeds of destruction soon -
War should be ended.

People like ice,
Dictators like lice,
Warmongers like mice,
What a price -
War should be ended.

People take heed,
Don't plant the seed
Which turns to weed,
That commits the deed.
So take heed -
War should be ended.

THE WELL

In the modern world
We have nearly everything;
Saucepans, cars and tellys,
And even golden rings.
We take it all for granted
And create a lot of waste;
When it comes to helping others,
We don't show forth our haste.

Nature's glorious treasures,
All through the world we tell;
What's the use of sun and rain.
When we haven't got a well.

We want a channel tunnel,
A supersonic 'plane;
We like to have our pleasures,
But curse the pouring rain;
When it comes to spending money,
it all goes down the drain
We never like to lose,
We always want to gain.

Nature's glorious treasures,
All through the world we tell;
What's the use of sun and rain,
When we haven't got a well.

There are countries such as Bangladesh.
Which haven't got much food,
They're dying of starvation,
Their implements are crude;
It's the same in India, Pakistan and Vietnam,
Cambodia, Nigeria, Sri Lanka, it's all the same.

Nature's glorious treasures,
All through the world we tell;
What's the use of sun and rain.
When we haven't got a well.

With all our great technology,
We ought to lend a hand,
To help them in their hour of need,
But not to take command
To help their crop rotation,
And irrigate their land,
To bring back cool, clear water,
And drive away the sand.

Nature's glorious treasures,
All through the world we tell;
What's the use of sun and rain,
When we haven't got a well.

We've got to work together,
There isn't very much time;
To leave them in their suffering
Would be the greatest crime.
Love thy neighbour as thyself,
That's what the Good Lord said,
It's time to get a move on,
Before our neighbour is dead.

Nature's glorious treasures,
All through the world we tell;
What's the use of sun and rain,
When we haven't got a well.

* * *

LITTLE FLY

Little fly upon the floor',
Why do you move towards the door.
When I drop this great big book,
It will surely change your luck.
Little fly upon the floor,
Oh dear, you are no more.

OUR PROTECTOR

Now we are together
On this brand new day
Through the night brought safely
We will soon be on our way
God is here beside us
Keeping harm at bay
Be our safe protector
And with us abide.

When we are in danger
He will hear our call
Rally us together
So that we may never fall
Lord our mighty Saviour
Father of us all
Be our safe protector
And with us abide.

WHEN

When . .
On some starry night,
I look into the heavens there,
And see mysteries in the skies,
Looking over time's immortal rays.

When . .
Short time you have had
To live amongst us here,
Yet now you live above us,
Watching here.

When ..
Time
Will bring us near again,
In everlasting company.
You and me, For all to see,
We shall meet
When.

When . . .
We shall be together,
Through long forgotten time;
We'll laugh and sing,
Then.

* * *

ONE SHORT

Have you seen it?
Have you seen it?
I had it yesterday,
I know I just can't find it,
What am I to say ?

Can you see it?
Can you see it?
Please help me understand;
Why can't I find it?
I had it in my hand.

It is really precious,
It's as pretty as a jewel;
I had it here this morning,
I left it
On the stool.

Oh goodness gracious,
Goodness gracious,
What am I to do?
I've got to take it tomorrow,
I'm getting in a stew.

Just a minute,
Just a minute,
I've had a terrible thought -
Ah, now I remember
We were one short!

* * *

TRAVEL ON

Across the foothills do I wander,
Lonely in despair;
I hope that I'll find happiness,
Someday when I get there.

I'm looking for something,
I'm looking for someone;
Just give me food and drink,
And then I'll travel on.

One day I met a woman
With long and silky hair;
She wanted me to marry her,
But I said I couldn't stay there.

I'm looking for something,
I'm looking for someone;
Just give me food and drink.
And then I'll travel on.

There must be a place for me,
If I could only find it;
But every time I get near to one,
Somebody seems to hide it.

I'm looking for something,
I'm looking for someone;
Just give me food and drink,
And then I'll travel on.

So then I'll keep on searching,
But you won't know where I've gone,
So don't look for me in the morning,
I'll just travel on.

* * *

WHAT'S IN A WORD?

What's in a word?
If it's "yes" it means
I will,
I do,
I am,
I can,
I would like to,
I want to.

If it's "no" it means
I won't,
I can't,
I wouldn't want to,
I'm not,
I shall not.

I shall not, what?
Shall not love -
Why not?
Why should I?
Because....

Love is love
Love is taking care of someone,
Love is joining in whatever they do,
Love is promising yourself to them always -
To cherish,
To obey - not necessarily,
That's a bit outdated,
But to honour anyway;
Love is not hate,
Hate is not love,
Love is love,
That's what's in a word.

ONE TOO MANY

Little light upon the ceiling
I often wonder what you're feeling
When I come home late at night
Feeling weary, merry, tight.
I sit and watch you reeling, reeling
And get the most peculiar feeling.

* * *

FLY

Part 2

We met a long time ago,
You took my hand
Led me through this land
Of forgotten time.
Yet I still wait
Waiting for you to come

Flying to the sky
On clouds just too high,
Sun shadows shining
Way up high,
Help me fly.

Night time is calling
As shadows come
Falling silently.
Astral belt
Light shines brightly
Take me high
Help me fly
Into the sky.

Lead me back home
In the morning.
Love has yet to meet
Could be any street
Hear you calling
Come, come
I see you there
Bright shining hair
Come take me high

Part 3

We fly over lands of gold
Feelings that are cold,
People that are old
Throughout the universe.
You take my hand
Guide me across the sand
A movement which is planned
Within the universe.
Love is real.

This is what I feel,
it can only heal,
Upon the universe.
Fly me into the sky,
Into the sky,
Fly me into the sky.
Into the sky,
Fly me high.

RHYTHM

The sea comes in.
The sea goes out.
The seasons change,
Monsoon and drought.

People go here.
People go there;
In regular patterns
Life does appear.

The noisy car,
The crowded bar,
Nowhere to park it;
A busy supermarket.

Busy city,
The country's pretty.
Regular patterns do emerge.
Almost like a funeral dirge.

But wait....
A sudden noise;
Disturbance;
A change.
The pattern slow, stops, listens.
Something unusual,
A discord,
Irregular.
What is it ?

The pattern of life changes,
The rhythm's gone.
Earthquake.
Natural disaster.
Disruption.
The rhythm changes.

No more,
No more,
Yet slowly 'tis all one rhyme
Yet slowly, and then more rapidly
The rhythm begins to beat again.

COUNTRY JACK

I breathe the country air,
My name is Country Jack,
I have no clothes to spare,
Just those upon my back.

All day long I sing along,
As happy as can be;
My name is Country Jack, my friend,
So come and follow me.

We plough the fields all day,
And merrymake all night;
Our life is always gay,
We work with all our might.

All day long I sing along,
As happy as can be;
My name is Country Jack, my friend,
So come and follow me.

So if your life is sad,
Come along with me;
It'll be oh so glad,
And happy you shall be.

All day long I sing along,
As happy as can be;
My name is Country Jack, my friend,
So come and follow me.

* * *

OUR GIFT

We must always use the gift
That our Father does provide
Never let our skills to drift,
Never let our talents glide.

Just like the servants of old,
Who were given pieces of gold,
Surely we must do our best
For God, who has set the test.

Through His own redeeming light,
We will join the glorious fight.
Worthy of his heavenly call,
On together go we all.

* * *

THE CHURCH

The church is sombre
The light is grey
People sit, or kneel and pray.
The vicar speaks a sermon
In voice both loud and clear
Deafening the people who're sitting near.
His words fly through emptiness
And in the air are heard
But the congregation do not comprehend a word:
Some are sleeping, some are sitting,
Some others just smirk.
Their thoughts echo across the church
This is easier than doing God's work.
Rejoice! For Christ lives!
And happy be ye all.
Yet the hymns, like some far off hope,
Sound more like a funeral.
Where are the young people
That used to come to church'?
They're not here because the words aren't clear.
They've been left in the lurch.
The words are not clear any more
The church cannot communicate,
And yet . . . far off
Young people throughout the world
Have seen the message
Change! Before it's too late.
No longer from the pulpit the dreary sermons pour,
But far off the people dance and sing
And Jesus they adore
He is no longer a figure in a book
Something worshipped from afar
From now on, he sings and dances
He is a Superstar.
Prepare ye the way of Jesus Christ,
John the Baptist said
So let us dance, sing
Lift up our hearts; be happy and smile
For Jesus is Not dead!

* * *

PEACE

What is peace
Give us peace
Peace is love
Peace is hope
Living together is peace,
Knowing that everything is well.

What is peace?
Give me peace.
Love is peace,
Hope is peace,
Peace is peace.

A POEM TO ALL DICTATORS AND TERRORISTS

Violence, bloodshed, hatred, distress;
The right to conquer, command, oppress,
To destroy creation of nature and love
Sent down to earth from heaven above.
War is your anthem,
Death is your song -
Don't sing it too loudly,
Your hour is not long.

* * *

QUEEN OF THE MILKY WAY

She flies over the country,
She flies across the sky.
Heaven is her home,
Her empire stands on high.

She flies high across the sky,
My love is queen of the milky way.

When love is in the balance,
And hate and death converge,
She brings to me such loving peace
To end the funeral dirge.

She flies high across the sky,
My love is queen of the milky way.

Some men speak of true love,
Others speak of hate.
I belong to you my love,
Please wait at the star gate.

She flies high across the sky,
My love is queen of the milky way.

We'll spend our lives together
In the heavens up above
The world shall never witness
A more eternal love.

We'll fly high across the sky,
And we'll be lovers in the milky way.

SECONDS, MINUTES, HOURS

Time presses on,
The seconds tick by -
Hours of waiting
For you and I.

In a moment we shall know,
This second is too long,
Happiness or sadness
Will be our next song.

As time goes by
We both grow old.
But our love is too hot
To ever grow cold.

Together we stay
As minutes tick away.
As seconds go by
Our love will never die.

Through minutes, seconds, hours.
We share each others joy;
Our love ,we know is ours,
Between this girl and boy.

* * *

MY TOWN

When I was young
I was proud of my town.
But now I've gone away,
But I can still dream about my town
On a sunny day.

Robin Hood our hero
And the Sheriff -
Such an evil man.
These are people of Nottingham.

The River Trent
And barge canals
A castle
On the hill.

Byron, the poet,
Lawrence, the writer,
Arkwright, the merchant,
King Ludd, the fighter.

It's different now -
The Trent is murky,
We don't eat pheasant -
We just eat turkey.

Thousands queuing
On the dole
Scanlon scores
The wining goal.

Super centres.
High rise flats.
Social security,
Millions of cats.

Some of it's good,
Some of it's bad,
Some of it makes you frown -
Nevertheless
It's home to me,
For this is my home town.

* * *

TO THE GIRL I ONCE LOVED

Her hair it flowed like silk,
Her manner was charming,
Her effect upon my character
Was really quite disarming.

Where'er she walked,
The grass stood still,
And daffodils sing
Upon the hill.

The moon and stars
Would shine at night,
Their radiance created
Silver light.

Her beauty still
Within my mind;
Seldom have I met
A girl of her mind.
She is gone now,
Yet I love her still -
It seems to me
I always will.

In bed at night,
My eyes I rubbed,
Crying for the girl
That once I loved

OH LORD

Oh Lord,
Help us to value friendship
And to cherish it:
The friendships we have made this week.
Another friendship we may make in the future;
But most of all, help us to remember
The special friendship we have with you -
And to cherish it always.

Amen.

* * *

THE LITTLE PIECE OF PAPER

If I had time and space,
I'd speak of love and the human race;
I would surely remark
On CIeo's love for Mark.
Other great loves there have been,
Some you may have seen,
Others you will ne'er forget
Like Romeo and Juliet.

But oh this piece of paper
Quickly begins to taper,
And I with haste must race
To use up all the space;
And yet things will have their way,
Sufficient it is to say
I love you.

* * *

Chapter 2
Heart Song (1978)

Alyn says: When God calls sometimes you have to wait. Having finished university and knowing that eventually I would train for ministry, it was a time of waiting, of experimenting with different kinds of work.

THE POET

This is the second magazine in which we cover more of the work of Alyn Haskey who started us in publishing disabled poets work.

An inspiration to all, Alyn Haskey is 26 years old, who, despite terrible handicaps, made it to Prestigious University of York, where he was studying History and Sociology. On March 3rd 1976 he won The Spastic Society's Achievement of the Year Award, for which he received a cheque for £250, plus a medal and silver cup.

Alyn, who is in a wheel-chair, has poor speech and cannot feed or dress himself. His only method of writing is by operating an electric typewriter by a stick held between his teeth.

However, he finished his University course in the normal three years, despite his handicap. From eleven to sixteen years of age Alyn was in a school for the educationally sub-normal children, but his achievements since those days are very impressive. He has won the Duke of Edinburgh's Bronze, Silver and Gold Awards, written songs, plays, poems and serial stories. When not studying Alyn paints, holding a brush between his teeth, arid he was sports writer for the University. He has won numerous prizes in the games and sports for the disabled.

Alyn was looked after by a member of the Community Service Volunteers, who has a room next to his at Alcuin College.

Since Alyn left University he took a short break before starting a course in Christian work, to prepare him for the life that the Lord has in store for him later on. He is now at St. John's College, Chilwell, Nottingham where he finds the work taking him to a far, fuller life than he ever imagined was possible.

ONE TOUCH   Dedicated to brother Dave,

One touch was all I needed
to set me free from sin,
One touch from Jesus,
and I let my Saviour in,

One touch from Jesus,
Can fill you with such love.
One touch from him,
Will give you blessings from above.

One touch from Jesus
Will give you a new life
One touch from the Saviour,
Will take away your pain and strife.

One touch from Jesus,
And the healing has begun,
One touch from the Lord,
And you've become a son.

Praise the SAVIOUR,
For what he's done for me,
One touch from Jesus,
Has really set me free.

One touch, One touch,
Ho will set you free,
One touch from Jesus,
Will last through eternity.

NEW

Everything is made new,
All the wonders of creation,
Changing day by day,
By the hand of God
Touching everything,
With His precious love,

The sun is rising,
Day begins
And glory shines around
The trees and flowers
Burst into life
Birds singing their sweet sounds.

The moon is shining,
And stars come out
The night is crisp and clear
The seasons change,
The colours blend
And He renews each year.

You touched my heart,
And life begins,
No longer blind, I see,
Your healing hand,
Renews my spirit
I'm growing and I'm free.

The weak gain strength,
The blind their sight,
By His love which is true
The lame, they walk,
The lost are found,
By Him are we made new.

* * *

SPRING SONG

Awaken,
The sun is shining,
New life begins,
Hear the birds sing,
Clouds glisten,
New life begins,

Dewy grass
Shines in the pouring rain
The Winter's gone,
The time has come,
For Spring to come again,

And we will walk together,
In the freshness
now the darkness
Has turned into light
As birds sing sweetly;
In the morning
And nature's glory
Comes into our sight.

We will sing of new beginnings,
As we look forward to the sun,
For the Glory of God
Is all around us,
We can share as we join as one

And as the morning comes,
We know the Lord has risen
And life begins anew
Come let us join together,
And welcome in the Spring,
It comes for me and you.

Awaken,
The sun is shining,
New life begins
For Winter has turned into Spring.

* * *

BLIND MANS BUFF

You're turning round in circles,
You want to play games with me,
As long as you keep your eyes
    closed,
You know you won't see.

You had a good time at the party,
Now it's coming to an end,
But you are going home alone now,
You haven't found a friend.

You think that life is a party,
Don't hurry now there's time
    enough,
But you just might miss the
    moment,
While you're playing Blind Man's
    Buff

You've heard the things I'm saying
    to you,
A thousand times before,
But every time He approaches,
You slam the door.

Can't you see that you are wrong,
And there's the question of your
    fate,
Smiles will turn to tears,
When you find that it's too late.

Someone wants to love you,
If you'll give Him half a chance,
The music that He'll give you,
Will set you free to dance.

* * *

DOCTOR DOCTOR

Doctor, doctor help me if you can,
Can't you see I'm a broken man,
I've been waiting for so long,
For someone to help me see
Doctor, doctor help me if you can

Open my eyes so I can see again,
Release my heart from this heavy
chain,
I need you now to come,
And lay your hands on me,
Doctor, doctor take away the pain

And the healer is coming by today,
Won't you reach out as he comes
down your way
He longs to set you free,
To be what you want to be,
So that you can start again.

Now my heart is free I can dance,
Your love has given me a second
chance,
Now each day begins a new,
And it all comes down to you,
Doctor, doctor I'm a new man.

* * *

RICH WORLD - POOR PEOPLE

Billy's in tears,
'Cos his money's all gone,
And He can't go out tonight
He earns his wages,
And blows it away,
Don't you know that ain't right

Mrs Johnson goes to town,
To buy a new coat,
It's got to be the best,
It's got to look good,
In front of the neighbours,
She's out to impress.

Don't you know that there are
people starving,
They haven't got enough to eat,
They're lying down on the hard ground
While you sit in your velvet seat.

Rich world, poor people,
Don't you think we've got it wrong
Don't you know they're
    getting angry,
Judgement's coming and it
    won't be long.

We spend all our tine
Trying to gain
The latest toy around,
But when it comes
To listen to others,
We don't hear a sound.

You know we don't own it
We're here to share it
That's what it's all about
People are hungry,
We've got the food,
Listen to them shout.

And we've got to get it right
Before it gets too late,
Of the food that's on the plate
To love our neighbour,
And share what we have
To quench burning hatred,
With a gentle flow of love.
* * *

LOVE FALL ON ME
Love fall on
Whenever I am sad,
Love fall on me
When things start turning bad
You know that I love you
And you are my friend
Pour down your love
And never let it never end.

Love fall on me
When life get's just too rough
Love fall on,
For I can't get enough
You died for me
And cast away all my chains
Pour down your love
And take away my pain.

Your love is true
And it will never end
I thank you Lord
For all the love you send.

Love fall on me
And change my tears to peace
Love fall on me
And let it never cease
I know You love me
And I love You
Love fall on me
And let it soak right through.
* * *

THE HARVESTER
MATTHEW 13:24-34
Oh children
Listen to the words
For the wind blows
And the time comes near,
The Harvester does approach.

If your fruit is good
Then you have no fear,
If your life is true
Then the way is clear,
If your corn is ripe
Then you will be reaped
When the Harvester does appear.

But if His words
Like seeds
Fall on rocky ground
And you grow like weeds
Then you will be found
In the fire,
You will be burnt
When the Harvester does appear.

Oh children
The time is nigh
Look unto the earth
Look up to the sky
For the Harvester
And his day on hand

All ye weeds
Now fear
For the time is near
All the corn,
Like yeast now rise
For the Lord of harvest
He is here.
* * *

SONG FOR YOU

I've got no need to hide
Or cover up my faith,
And I won't listen to you
When you tell me it's a disgrace,
From now on I'm living in a different place.

You say I'm misguided
And I don't know what is true,
But when I look into your eyes
I have my doubt about you,
Are you so sure of the things you do.

You say it's all illusions
And that you ought to know
One of these days you're going to realise
That it isn't so don't you know.

You say I ought to know better
With the intelligence I've got,
That it comes down to me
And I should push myself a lot,
But your words to me don't seem very hot.

The angry bell rips the silence
And there's no time left to wait,
All the things you doubted have come
And now it's much too late.

Well I've listened hard
To every word you said,
And it seems to me
That you think God is dead
But if he is you tell me who's
The love I keep hearing in my head.

TODAY

Sunday morning,
In the garden,
Mary, at the tomb,
Disciples lost,
Where to go?
Everything is gloom.

The tomb is empty,
Gardener stands by,
Where could He be?
He's living,
He is alive,
We're free.

He's risen,
He's alive for evermore,
He's come to free us,
To open heaven's door,

He is risen,
He is risen,
Now we shall be free,
He is risen, He is risen,
And he comes for you and me.

He's alive today,
And He reigns for evermore
And He longs to live within us
And to show us the way.

He's alive today,
His spirit fills our heart,
Come praise the living Lord,
Who gives us a new start.

He's alive, He's alive, today,
He's alive today,
And He wants to set us free,
His love will last forever,
And he comes for you and me.
He's alive today
And he'll reign for evermore,
So open up your heart
He's knocking at the door
He's alive, He's alive, today.

* * *

VALIUM BLUES

Well good grief, What's wrong with me,
I'm not shaking like a leaf,
Or bending like a tree,
I don't feel ill,
But I'd better take a pill
To help me sit still.

I was down in Wales and He said to me,
Look at me, I can set you free,
I said, O.K You're the boss;
He said, Throw away;
I said "What did You say?"
He said, "You can do it!"
I said, "Will I get through it?"
He said, "Throw away your pills, and cast away your ills!"

So I thought about it, He said, "Go on, try it!
You can' t talk about Me if you can't trust Me."
I said, "You know that's true"
So I threw them away and to this very day
I feel really free,
So if you've got ills throw away your pills and
Get hooked on Jesus instead.

* * *

AMAZING LOVE

Amazing love how can it be
What you have done to me,
My spirit now is lifted
My captive heart is free.

You came to me
One dark and stormy night
You calmed my fears and sorrow,
You said that it would be alright.

As the day went by
You showed me things I'd never seen before,
Each day new golden treasures
You laid outside my door.

As the time has passed
I've come to know you as you touch my heart,
For you have given everything
Right from the start.

* * *

THE TIME OF THE BEAST

He came like a stranger
Bringing hope for the world,
All the answers he had in his hand
But instead he misled us,
And took away our freedom
From the beginning he had it all
    planned.

It's the time of the beast
It's the end of peace,
And I don't know if anyone will
    survive
It's the time of the beast,
Watch his power increase
There'll be no one left alive.

He wants your mind now
So that you will worship him
He's got a number just waiting for
    you
And if you want to live,
Then you've got to give
He knows everything that you do.

And there's no place to hide
His eyes are all around you,
He wants to possess you
To keep you from the truth,
For he knows that his time is
    running out.

The message you got
You've heard a thousand times before,
But you wouldn't stop and listen to reason
But you've made your bed,
And you'll have to lie upon it
Who knows how long it will be till the end of his season.

* * *

PAPERCHASE

Words fly up and down,
Letters all around,
Paper dreams,
Flowing streams,
I look into your eyes,
Feel the rhythm,
Moving,
Follow,
Chasing,
Paper flying,
Words chasing,
Sunshine,

Chasing,
Follow,
Your eyes shining,
Paper words,
Paper dreams,
Chasing paper chasing paper,
Streams? Streams?
Rhythm Faster,
Paper chasing,
Chasing? Chasing,
Paperchasing,
Paperchase.

* * *

CONSEQUENCES
PART I

She leaves the kitchen,
She's on her way to town,
To meet her lover,
She's so afraid
What if my husband ever finds out".

Two men walking,
Staggering up a hill
They've been drinking,
Why not?
There is nothing left to look
    forward to.

He's in prison again,
Could be life,
So many times,
What can be done,
No one seems to care about you.

But it's only consequences,
Of a world that's lost it's head
What was good has now turned
    rotten,
It's only consequences of a world,
Without Jesus.

PART 2

Somewhere in the darkest light,
A cry for help,
A world that's lost,
Its passions tossed
It's looking for the light.

Two thousand years ago,
The Lord of life came down,
They suspected,
They rejected,
And thorns were his crown.

There has to be an answer,
To this misery,
The pain,
The rain,
Who can set us free,

PART 3

If you look for him,
You'll find him.
He'll take away your pain.
You can have
A point to life,
You can start again.

There's no need for you to live,
The kind of life you do,
Follow him, every day,
And he will lead you through.

And it's only consequences
Of the new life that you will lead,
You will find the good things meant for you
It's only consequences of life
Spent with Jesus.

PRISONER

You can think what you want to
As long as you do what I say,
If you keep your beliefs to yourself,
You're gonna be OK
But if you step out of line
You know I'll put you away.

You know we've got a fine country,
As long as we all do what is right,
We don't live in the darkness,
'Cos ideals shine in the light,
And if you don't agree with us,
There'll be a knock on the door at midnight.

Don't you know you're a prisoner,
But living at liberty,
But don't get on the wrong side,
Or you'll find yourself on a tree,

We've got peace and quiet,
Free of love and hope,
We've got people to help you,
If you just can't cope,
So, why don't you join us?
Don't just sit there and mope.

I want to be free
And believe what I want to,
Don't tell me what to do or say,
You know you can't hold me,
Or stop me talking
It's getting near to Judgment Day.

I'm a prisoner, a prisoner,
You can't hold me down,
I'm going to lose my chains,
And gain a precious crown.

You tell me I'm free,
To do just what I want to,
As long as I do what is right,
But I'm not going to stand,
And let you mislead them,
Pretending that darkness is light.

So you can't stop me,
From telling the truth,
No matter what you try to do,
Don't you realise,
That time is passing,
And your day is almost through.

PUPPET

Narrator
Once there was a man,
Who searched for freedom
He looked high and low
Looking for his goal,
But he couldn't find it.
So he broke away
Left his father far behind,
Went in search of riches,
Trying to find his freedom,
Break away, break away.

Puppet
Over hills and valleys,
Walking in the sun
Searching for the things I wanted,
Freedom I had won,
Was it in the sunrise
Or by shining light of moon,
Happiness is what I seek,
Hope I find it soon.
And in the distance a caravan,
Could this be the answer.

Mephisto
I am the great Mephisto,
I will give you everything,
Come and work for me,
I'll make you a king,
All my heart desires,
I will give to you,
I'll show you what to do.

Gold and silver,
Rich and wealthy,
I'll give you more and more,
High society, good parties,
Lots of friends are yours.

Narrator
Day after day,
He worked for his master,
And it seemed that all was well,
Having cars,
High living,
Power, fame and wealth.

But at night,
He couldn't sleep
He could find no peace
False friends
And great disillusion,
Pain that would not cease.

Puppet
I am in darkness
The world is dimming,
I don't want to dance and sing,
But when he calls,
I have to answer
When he pulls the string.

When the music starts
I know he's coming
To make me dance and sing,
Can't resist
He got the power
To pull my strings,

And in the darkness,
My soul is crying
Won't someone rescue me?
Please help me
You know I'm dying,
I want to be free.

Narrator
And as he sits in his cell
He knows he's going to hell,
Is there anyone who'll save him?

Puppet
A voice called,
A man upon a cross
Come unto me,
And I will give you life,
What's this I see,
And he's calling me,
To go with him
There are wounds in his hands,
I just don't understand,
But He's calling me to go with him.

And as I look at him,
I've seen that face before,
I can't believe it,
It's my father,

Narrator
And he's calling towards him,
And his chains just fall away.

Puppet
I am Free
I am Free!

* * *

PILGRIMS SONG
Travelling down this lonely road,
Carrying a heavy load,
How I wish I had a friend
When will this journey end?

It seems I started long ago,
But the journey's much too slow,
Haven't gone very far
Just like reaching for a star.

And it's hard to carry on moving
And many times I have looked back,
And my body aches from head to toe
As if I've just come off a rack.

So I've got to keep on moving,
To keep my courage up I'll sing,
Though it hurts deep inside,
There'll be a turning of the tide.

Now my progress seems much slower,
As I journey up this hill,
I'm not sure that I can make it
I don't think I ever will.

But as I struggle there's a hand upon me,
And in this distance I see a light,
And as I pull myself over the top,
What a beautiful sight.

Welcome to the city of your dreams,
Glad you've made it home at last,
Now you can look to the future,
And drive away the past.

Come through the gates of the city,
And take the life that's within,
Now you're home forever,
And your new life will begin.

I didn't think I could make it,
But standing here I feel so good,
And there in the middle was the man who helped me,
His hands and feet still scarred from the wood.

He took my hand and said welcome,
I've been waiting for you,
Every tear and pain has been counted,
Now you're home there's nothing more to go through.

* * *

THE SUN WILL RISE AGAIN

In the valley of shadow,
I am all alone.
Wondering what's gone wrong.
All the hope that I had,
Have somehow gone bad,
Now I sing my sad song.

But in the morning,
There'll be an end to pain,
The clouds will fly,

Why am I so lonely,
Is there any hope?
Just what am I supposed to do?
Then I saw you in the distance,
You opened up your arms,
And I saw that your love was true.

And now the darkness has disappeared,
My heart sings when you are near,
You've changed my life and set me free,
In your presence is where I want to be.

* * *

KINGDOM COME

Look look around you,
Can't you see the signs?
Something's coming,
In our hearts, in our minds.

You can feel it in the air now,
You can see it on the ground,
Open up your eyes,
Look it's all around,
Kingdom come.

All the pain and sorrow
Will vanish from our sight,
There's a new tomorrow,
When darkness turns to light.

And the prophets told us all about it,
That the time will come when we'll
be free,
And the sounds of joy will be heard,
A time of love for you and me.

Is it round the corner?
Is it on the street?
Is it on the faces,
Of the people that we meet?

YOU

I was walking by the river,
When I saw you coming towards me.
You were walking on the water
You were holding out your hand
All I did was turn away, I am not worthy.

You died upon a cross,
You rose up from the grave,
You gave the victory to me.
I would not listen,
But still you kept on talking,
Now I'm beginning to see.

You told me of the future,
You told me of the past
That you would be rejected,
And the promise that would last
All I did was turn away, I am not worthy.

You take away my troubles,
You wash away my sins.
And now new life begins,
And I turn to you, for you made me worthy.

SHED YOUR GENTLE LOVE

Shed your gentle love on me,
And lift me when I'm down,
You have the power to change me,
So I may wear a crown
Take my heart, it's yours now,
I want to be like you,
I'm waiting now, shed your love on me.

So after I have let you down,
When I could have done more,
Now I'm begging on my knees,
Please don't shut the door on me,
I long to give you glory,
To walk closer to you,
I'm waiting now shed your love on me.

Please won't you help me,
I need your gentle hand,
I want to walk beside you,
In the life that you have planned.

Take me as you find me,
I won't hide from you
I long to be surrounded,
By your love which is so true,
I'll give you everything my Lord,
If you will set me free,
I'm waiting now, shed your love on me

STAND

There's so many different people,
Trying to tell me what to do,
Fill my head with stories,
Which I know just aren't true.
They try to mesmerise me,
To fit me in a box,
And when I just don't listen,
They threaten me with locks.

Jesus won't you help me stand,
Keep me in the palm of your hand.
When the world tries to change me,
Help me keep my eyes on you,
Jesus won't you help me to stand.

The things that they are saying,
They ring inside my head.
It doesn't matter how you live,
You know that God is dead.
They try to pressure me,
To make me toe the line,
But I know that I'm different,
And you can't own my mind.

And sometimes it's hard to carry on,
When I'm all alone against the wild.
But then when your love comes around me,
And I want to shout your name out loud.

You're all I live for,
And when the times get rough,
Your strength will come upon me,
And that's more than enough.
Jesus when you are near me,
I feel safe in your hands,
The world can come against me,
For you I will stand.

YOUR WILL

I won't do it!
Why should I go through it
Why should I be the one
To do what must be done?

There must be others
Much more worthy,
For this task
Than am I?

I am so scared
It is so hard,
To do your will
And yet I know
That there is
No other one,
To do your will
That must be done to
save the world.

I will do it!
Lead me to it,
I will do it
For the ones I love.

Take me now
Before I change,
My mind
And go.

And through it all
I see the love you have to offer,
Your will is done
Your Kingdom come,
Now and forever.

And through it all
Through tears and pain,
If you should ask
For such a task,
I'd die again.

* * *

DOUBT

You think you've got it all worked out,
And that you haven't got a doubt,
You can't believe He died for you,
You just can't see how it could be true.

Blind eyes can't see,
Deaf ears won't listen,
But what about the night,
Are you sure you've got it right.

You want to live your life as your own,
And yet you're afraid of being on your own,
You still refuse to believe that He can help you,
But deep inside you don't know what you're going to do.

Don't you know that Jesus died for you,
And He can give you a love which is so true,
Won't you stop and listen to what I say,
He can help you to find the real way.

You're in a corner by yourself,
You have a fear of being left on the shelf,
You want to scream, you want to shout,
'Cause your mind is full of fear and doubt.

And in the darkness,
Your mind is running wild,
Things were simple,
When you were a child,
But complications,
Give you sleepless nights,
And you're not sure,
If you're right.

ONE DAY SOON

There's a bluebird flying high,
It's wings touch the sky,
And I want to follow,
There's a sound in the air,
Which isn't really there,
And it sings down in the hollow,
And my heart is so free,
But my body waits for me.
And I will fly,
Rise up on eagle's wings,
No longer tied by strings,
One day soon.
It will not be too long,
'Til I sing a different song,
And the world will ring with
    laughter,
And the sun will shine all day,
There'll be blue instead of grey,
And love will reign forever after,
For His love has broken the chain,
And taken all the pain.

FREEDOM FIGHTER

The chains have been broken
The gates are open wide.
He has released us,
When on the cross He died.

The sins that once held you
He now drives from sight
Your conscience is clear now
As day replaces night.

The freedom fighter he has come
To break down the door of death
    and sin
He's conquered the jailer of
    oppression
Now we're free to follow.

His love is forever
His life will never end
His joy will surround you
When you become His friend.

You can be free now
Of all that holds you down,
Swap those heavy chains
For a shiny crown.

Jesus is waiting
For you to come to Him
Take the road to freedom
A new life will begin.

I AIN'T NOTHING WITHOUT YOU

When I'm falling down
You lift me up,
When I'm running low
You fill my cup.

When I look at you I know it's true,
I ain't 'nothing without you.

You touch my eyes
And now I can see,
You touch my heart
And set me free.

I'm running as fast as I can
But I ain't getting any place,
I need to stop
And look into your face.

Your love is with me
Each and every day,
I'm going to follow you
Which is the only way.

ACQUITTED

The judge and the jury
Had made up their mind,
And although he did nothing
Guilty was the verdict they would find.

They took him from the city
To a nearby hill
An innocent man was hung there
Him they wanted to kill.

It's the crime of the universe
And I can't understand why,
Such an innocent victim had to die.

As I watched him dying
In the burning sun,
I heard these words come from his lips
Forgive them they don' t know what they have done.

Now I am free from all that holds me down
A new way of life is what I have found,
The fears that were over me
have now disappeared.

I can face the judge with hope and confidence
Who can accuse me I have my defence,
The future looks bright
My name has been cleared

It's the crime of the universe
Now I understand why,
He took my place
When he was led out to die.

GOOD TIME CITY

Living from day to day,
You know it's the only way,
Gonna have fun tonight,
Drink till the morning light,
In the morning I'll feel bad,
But that don't matter.

It's good time city,
Everything going fine
But when you get to the end of every day,
You'll find it's a waste of time.

Working from Monday till Friday
Got to earn enough to have some fun,
But when it comes to the week end,
Gonna lay out in the sun,
Every week is the same
It don't get any better.

And I'd like my life to be much better,
But I just can't find any peace of mind,
I look all around me, see people who are happy,
They've got the joy I just can't find.

Tomorrow and the day after,
Will it always be the same,
Can there ever be a new beginning,
Don't you think it's just a shame,
My life just drifting by,
It's moving faster and faster.

* * *

TAKING CARE

Who sees that the sun shines every morning?
Who sees that the stars come out at night?
Whose hand turns summer into autumn?
And when winter is gone brings in spring's new life?

And you tell me that it's just coincidence,
That there's no pattern to all the things we see,
But I know there are loving hands upon us
And there's someone taking care of you and me.

In your sadness you feel all alone now,
Is there someone who really cares for me?
Who can change the lonely life I'm living?
And from darkness and fears can really set me free.

Don't you know the answers to your questions
Are very close at hand?
Look around and see the one who made you,
See the purpose to your life that he has planned.

Jesus died that you might live forever,
Taking all your worries and your sin,
Now the gates of life stand open and ready,
So that you may enter in.

Then you see that there is no coincidence,
And you'll know that you are free,
For those loving hands have told it you,
That they are taking care of you and me.

WHERE HAVE YOU GONE?
It's two in the morning,,
Waiting for the dawning,
I am on my own,
I am so alone,
Where have you gone?

How did I offend you,
How can I amend you,
Don't leave me here,
My soul is bare,
Where have you gone?

Where have you gone
Why have you forsaken me?
I guess I know how Jesus felt,
Won't you please let your anger melt?
Where have you gone?

The dawn is breaking,
My heart is aching,
I am truly sorry,
I am on my knees,
Where have you gone?

In the morning light,
I know you're right,
Please forgive me,
For now I see,
Where have you gone?

Now your love surrounds me,
The more your anger hounds me,
You are still here,
Gone is my fear,
You are my Lord.

* * *

Chapter 3
Armageddon's calling (1981)

Alyn says: The world became smaller as I travelled in this country and also to the USA. It was the year I was picked for England to race and it was a time of hope, finishing college and waiting to see the next step.

Foreword

This is Book Three of poetry by Alyn Haskey, the well known disabled poet from Nottingham.

Since his last book, Alyn has been on television and spent some time in America giving talks to various groups over there.

Also his poetry has been acclaimed by critics as being some of the best produced work done at the present time.

He has bookings to give talks all over the country again this year, and is willing to do more, if asked, by any group wanting his services in this field.

WAIT TILL TOMORROW

You look at me as if I'm mad,
You may think I'm a fool;
You say, where are the dreams you had,
How can you be so cool?

Fairy tales don't happen now
And there's nothing you can do.
That may be your experience
But I know it's not true

Though today is cloudy,
And my heart is touched with sorrow,
I know my dreams will all come true.
Wait till tomorrow.

Sometimes we're afraid to dream
When there is little hope
But there is one who loves us
When we cannot cope.

Foundations crumble easily
Unless they' re built on stone.
his death has made me live again
His promise is now my own.

Though today is cloudy,
And my heart is touched with sorrow,
I know my dreams will all come true.
Wait till tomorrow.

That's why I keep on hoping;
There's nothing he can't do.
His love destroys my doubt and fear
And he can do the same for you.

Though today is cloudy,
And my heart is touched with sorrow,
I know my dreams will all come true.
Wait till tomorrow.

THE AGE OF THE GUN

Take a life,
Save a life,
You'd better run,
Peace has gone,
Law is broken,
It's the age of the gun.

An eye for an eye,
Tooth for tooth,
The strongest shall win,
The things of value
Have disappeared
It's the age of sin.

This is the age of the gun,
And there's nowhere left you can run,
But this part of time is running out,
And soon you'll hear the shout,
Here comes the Son.

Death and dying
Will fade away.
Sorrow will cease;
Weapons of hate
Will be destroyed
Come the age of peace.

This is the age of the gun,
And there's nowhere left you can run,
But this part of time is running out,
And soon you'll hear the shout,
Here comes the Son.

THE JOKER

He thinks that life is funny
That everything's a joke
But the laughter will turn to tears
And the punchline will make him choke

He never takes anything seriously
Or listens to anyone
He fills up his life with practical jokes
Till one day he will find it's all gone

He spends his life in mockery
Of anything that's true
And when it comes to reality
He hasn't got a clue

He never takes anything seriously
Or listens to anyone
He fills up his life with practical jokes
Till one day he will find it's all gone

There will come a time when the laughter stops
And tears will fill his eyes;
His fun and joy were all pretence,
His life was built on lies.

He never takes anything seriously
Or listens to anyone
He fills up his life with practical jokes
Till one day he will find it's all gone

WAY BACK

I must be completely out of my head
sitting here listening to you;
You say your situations hopeless
But I know that's not true

You're pouring out all your sorrows
Telling me that you can't cope,
But you refuse to listen to me
When I tell you that there is hope

Sitting here on desolate row,
You've gone as far as you con go,
But all I want you to know
Is - there's a way back

You used to live In luxury,
When everything was going right,
But now your day is filled with tears
And fears dominate your night

Sitting here on desolate row,
You've gone as for as you can go,
But all I want you to know
Is - there's a way back.

There's a man who gave his life for you
On a cross of knotted wood
And even in the darkest night
He can turn bad into good.

Sitting here on desolate row,
You've gone as for as you can go,
But all I want you to know
Is - there's a way back.

HEAVEN TONIGHT

Everybody's looking for a way to be happy
They're all hoping that it'll turn out right
Don't you realise the answer before your eyes
Look and see, you could find heaven tonight

You've tried every door and they don't open,
You keep on searching everywhere
Stop and look around - can't you hear the sound?
He wants to tell you that he's really there.

And the path you tread
Leads nowhere you'll find
Don't you take a look,
Don't close up your mind ,
For the peace that you're after
Is there within your sight
If you turn around,
You can find heaven tonight

There's someone who really wants to love you
If you will only give up your fight
His arms are open wide for you to come inside
Are you ready to find a heaven bright?

PRAYER SONG

Let your light shine
Come close to me tonight;
Let your love surround me
And I will be alright
I need you near me
To turn away my fright
Let your light shine tonight

Let your joy flow
Through me every day
Reach out to others
As I go on my way
Let me be yours
Speak through what I say
Let your joy flow today.

I am yours, now and forever
You have drawn me to yourself
Keep me close whatever may
                happen
I know for me you died

Let your peace come
Wherever I may go
Help me tell the world
What it needs to know
In all I do
Let your love show
Let your peace come forever.

* * *

DREAMVILLE

Take a trip down the years,
When life was worth living
When there was happiness,
Less taking, more giving.

Sweet music flowing down,
Songs of yesterday;
A dream world of fantasy
Where everything's OK

Come tonight, lay your money down
You can find fulfilment in a dream,
A life that's filled with sweetness
                and sugar
Topped with milky ice cream.

Turn your back upon the world
And make it disappear,
Close your eyes to reality,
Don't let it get too near

Come tonight, lay your money down
You can find fulfilment in a dream,
A life that's filled with sweetness and sugar
Topped with milky ice cream.

Let the days slip away,
Here's a place for you to hide
Ignore the voice that's calling you,
Keep it locked inside

Come tonight, lay your money down
You can find fulfilment in a dream,
A life that's filled with sweetness and sugar
Topped with milky ice cream.

* * *

COVER GIRL SMILE

I saw your face
Shining brightly as the sun,
Reaching out to me
Come and join your fun

In my heart there's a question all the while
What lies behind your cover girl smile?

The life you lead
Seems to be so fast
And I believe
You think it's going to last

In my heart there's a question all the while
What lies behind your cover girl smile?

Refrain: And how many tears do you cry at night?
And how many times do you wish you could be right?
There's a way to find out what is true
And someone who loves you

So when you're tired
Have had enough of running round
Open up your heart
To the love that can be found.

In my heart there's a question all the while
What lies behind your cover girl smile?

* * *

BEGINNINGS

When the snow falls down in August
When the sun doesn't show in June
Then you know the long-forgotten promises
Will come to pass very soon

And it seems to me that the world is upside down
And all the things we rely on lie shattered on the ground
So many questions and we haven't got a clue
And I begin to see it's true

So many things seem to change today
And I'm not sure where I'm going
Ways that seem right end in disaster
I'm scared to face what each new day will bring

And it seems to me that the world is upside down
And all the things we rely on lie shattered on the ground
So many questions and we haven't got a clue
And I begin to see it's true

I've heard there's a way to face the future
There isn't any anguish, doubt or fear
And there is nowhere left to hide - now I must decide
Seasons change; the time is drawing near.

And it seems to me that the world is upside down
And all the things we rely on lie shattered on the ground
So many questions and we haven't got a clue
And I begin to see it's true

BABYLON

Part 1   Come down to the mystical city
Come and have fun tonight
You can dance your life away
Till the morning light
In Babylon
You can have fun tonight

There are wondrous sights to see
You won't believe your eyes
All truth is meaningless
They only deal in lies
In Babylon
It doesn't pay to be wise

No one will ever shake her
Foundations solid in the ground
But tonight in the mystical city
There's a strange and worrying sound
In Babylon
The walls are falling down

Part 2   The great city has been broken
Never more to rise
The sword of truth with swift vengeance
Puts an end to lies
From Jerusalem
Shines the everlasting light

HILLS REJOICE!

Hills, rejoice to see your Saviour come
The time is near when we shall all go home
For the night is over and the new day is here
Hills, rejoice to see your saviour come

For many years we have struggled on
In darkest shadow, waiting for the Son
Now he comes as he promised
To bring the time of peace
Hills, rejoice to see your Saviour come

Hills, lift up your voice, come, dance and sing
On the mountain stands our Saviour King
He reigns for ever and none can stop him now
Hills, lift up your voice, come, dance and sing.

ROUGH JUSTICE

Everyone is equal
At least that's what they say
Then how come the rich get richer
While the poor live from day to day?
If you've got the muscle
You can fight for your rights
But those who haven't got a voice
Have the hardest fight

Rough justice, you think you've got it right
But you're using only half your sight
And there's gonna be a time when you'll find out you were wrong.

Open your eyes now
And you'll begin to see
Don't leave it to others
It's up to you and me
There's no one else
To do what must be done
We've got to get moving
Before the time has gone

Rough justice, you think you've got it right
But you're using only half your sight
And there's gonna be a time when you'll find out you were wrong.

Refrain: Jesus came to show us how to live
We should be like him and give, give, give

When Jesus returns
He's going to want to know
If we've obeyed him
Then with him we shall go

Justice, love and freedom
Are what he came to bring
And we are his servants
So that all may live in him.

Rough justice, you think you've got it right
But you're using only half your sight
And there's gonna be a time when you'll find out you were wrong.

WINTER OF DISCONTENT

Howling winds blowing in the city
Everywhere you look there ain't no pity
Snow is falling, never seems to end
Heart-breaking images drive you round the bend

Standing in the rain, wondering where your dreams went
Can't last much longer in this winter of discontent

Peace and fulfilment never seem to come
A forgotten stranger miles from home
City streets seem so dark and grey
You're always hoping there's a better way

Standing in the rain, wondering where your dreams went
Can't last much longer in this winter of discontent

Listen to the music playing in your head
If things don't change soon, might as well be dead
Life is a joke and the humour's sick
In the middle of a wall, like another brick

Standing in the rain, wondering where your dreams went
Can't last much longer in this winter of discontent

Refrain: But you can change
If that's what you want
So don't let anyone
Tell you you can't

Hey, you in the corner, it's time to start anew
Nothing is fixed but it all depends on you
Open your eyes and then you'll see
That life has meaning and you can be free

You can have his life, that's why he was sent
And he will come and end your winter of discontent

BABY, LOVE MUST COME SOME TIME

You've been looking for love that cannot fail
You've been hoping for a dream that cannot last
But like the sands on the beach
It slips through your fingers fast

And you're hoping it will work out fine
Baby, love must come sometime

Sometimes you feel so sad and lonely
You wish that it would end
But there's no one you can talk to
For you need more than a friend

And you're hoping it will work out fine
Baby, love must come sometime

Refrain: You've been looking for a lover
One day you'll discover
That he's only a prayer away
And he's calling to you
With a love that's true
That can turn your night into day

Why don't you open your eyes and look around
He knows the way you feel
Stop all your pretending
And find a love that's real

And you're hoping it will work out fine
Baby, love must come sometime

* * *

HEAR MY CRY

My God, my God
Why have you forsaken me?
My enemies are all around me
My body aches
And I hear them mocking
Won't you hear my cry

But still I will praise your name
For your mercy is ever the same

My God, my God
You have always been my shield
Don't let me be dismayed
For your love is forever
And I trust in you
And I know that you hear my cry

But still I will praise your name
For your mercy is ever the same

* * *

NOT YET

I would like to roam along the sea shore
To dance, to skip, to jump
To ride a horse, to kick a ball
To use my hands for others.
Not yet.

I'd like to sing the songs of joy
Play music on my guitar
To have a voice both loud and clear
To take the message far.
Not yet.

I'd like to be like Jesus
To never go astray
To have an answer to all the questions
I meet from day to day.
Not yet.

Sometimes the frustration brings me near to tears
Then my mind is restless, filled with doubt and fears
Yet there's a voice inside me who renews my hope
Turning doubt to certainty and with him I can cope

There's no other way to live
Only by his grace
One day all the things I hope for
I will see before my face.
And no more Not yet.

GOODBYE 'TIL THE NEXT TIME

The time we had together
Has gone so fast
The things we look forward to
Are in the past
Although it's hard
To say goodbye
We needn't feel sad
And here's the reason why

Goodbye 'til the next time
Don't forget to call
We're looking forward to the day
When we don't have to part at all

The sun shines so brightly
And it's a beautiful day
But the rain seems to come
When we're far away
But I know in my heart
We're together all the time
And when the troubles come
I'm still feeling fine

Goodbye 'til the next time
Don't forget to call
We're looking forward to the day
When we don't have to part at all

No, we cannot tell
When we'll meet again
And in anticipation
There's and aching pain
But I know that some day
Our lives will be as one
And we will stay forever
In the presence of the Son

Goodbye 'til the next time
Don't forget to call
We're looking forward to the day
When we don't have to part at all

ONLY YOU

Only you can heal the sorrow
When it gets too much to bear
And when I call your name
I know you're always there
Whether I'm happy
Or even when I'm sad
Only you know just how I feel

Only you can pick me up
When I've fallen down
You've changed my robes of mourning
For a joyful shining crown
And when I'm feeling lonely
And my friends have gone away
Only you can change the night into day

And sometimes friends around me
Don't seem to understand
They only see the funny side of me
They can't feel the frustration
Or the tears I cry inside
For they're the things
We almost want to hide

Only you can fill my life with calm
When the sea gets rough
You never let me get too tired
You know when I've had enough
And you know when I get restless
And you know when I'm down
Only you can touch my life and turn it round

And sometimes friends around me
Don't seem to understand
They only see the funny side of me
They can't feel the frustration
Or the tears I cry inside
For they're the things
We almost want to hide

You have called me to your kingdom
You've made me live again
You've taken all my sin
And all the pain
And when the road is hard
I know you're there beside me
Seeking out a path for me to go.

Only you can be the reason
As I struggle day by day
For the trials and jubilations
That I meet along the way
And when the journey's over
Then I will see your face
Only your love can see me through.

* * *

MAYDAY 666

Blood and destruction, total disruption
And the clock is telling the time
We've been misled, soon we'll be dead
And we thought it would work out fine

Mayday 666,
We are in a fix
Can somebody help us?

Now it begins, wage of our sins
There's no way we'll be left alone
The time is right, using his might
He has control of the throne

Mayday 666,
We are in a fix
Can somebody help us?

Refrain:
The darkness is all around us
And he wants to control the mind
Our eyes have been closed
As he made all his moves
Now it's too late we will find

Death will reign, constant pain
And you know it need not have been
For we should have heard the one who gave the word
But we'll have to bear it till the end of the scene

Mayday 666,
We are in a fix
Can somebody help us?

* * *

CASH ON THE NAIL

Fire falling from the sky
Don't it want to make you cry
He is the ransom
And we have our freedom

Thirty pieces of silver
The human race for sale
The price has been quoted
Cash on the nail

He wants your soul now
Before him you must bow
Empty promises he'll give to you
His lies will sound true

Thirty pieces of silver
The human race for sale
The price has been quoted
Cash on the nail

Bondage is what you have to bear
And he doesn't really care
But the price has already been paid
And the carpenter in the tomb was laid

Thirty pieces of silver
The human race for sale
The price has been quoted
Cash on the nail

And you're free
You have got a choice
Close your ears to the lies
And hear a different voice

There's no need for you to be in pain
You're redeemed, so throw away your chains
Freedom is what he has bought
No longer in the web are you caught

Thirty pieces of silver
The human race for sale
The price has been quoted
Cash on the nail
* * *

SO GOOD TO BE ALIVE

It's good to be alive
And to think how good you are
Joy within my heart
And I really want to thank you Lord

I wake up and see the Son
Every single day
It doesn't really matter to me
If it's cloudy or grey

It's good to be alive
And to think how good you are
Joy within my heart
And I really want to thank you Lord

And if there's trouble I don't mind
When I look to you
Your love is all around me
And you'll see me through

It's good to be alive
And to think how good you are
Joy within my heart
And I really want to thank you Lord

Whether the sun is shining bright
And to think how good you are
Joy within my heart
And I really want to thank you Lord
* * *

TOE THE LINE!

What are all those strange ideas
That keep coming from your head?
I think you'd better try and forget them
Before you become mislead

Got no room for an individual
So you'd better change your mind
Or you'll find that you're alone now
So you'd better toe the line

Stop trying to be different
Don't you know we're all the same
If you keep on with this thinking
You'll be the one to take the blame

Got no room for an individual
So you'd better change your mind
Or you'll find that you're alone now
So you'd better toe the line

So just have a bit of sense now
Don't try to make a fuss
It's time for you to make your mind up
Are you with Him or with us

Got no room for an individual
So you'd better change your mind
Or you'll find that you're alone now
So you'd better toe the line

Part 2

I'm not going to listen to you
I know that you're wrong
All the lies you keep telling
Like some old song

Try to put me in a box
But you know you won't succeed
I've come upon the truth
Now my mind has been freed

Got no room for an individual
So you'd better change your mind
Or you'll find that you're alone now
So you'd better toe the line
You can't hold me anymore
There's no use in you crying
Your power has been broken
I won't change my mind

48

Refrain:
I'm not going to toe the line
He has freed my mind
You're just wasting your time
I'm not going to toe the line

* * *

FREEDOM ON THE WING

Fly like an eagle
Soar into the sky
Nothing there can stop me
Flying way up high

Can't you hear my heart sing
Freedom, freedom on the wing.

They try to hold me down
They try to make me stay
I've found the way to freedom
It gets better every day

Can't you hear my heart sing
Freedom, freedom on the wing.

Refrain:
People think I'm tied down
When they look at me
Appearances are deceptive
Jesus has set me free

The day is coming
When I will leave your sight
Freedom is forever
In the glory of his light

Can't you hear my heart sing
Freedom, freedom on the wing.

* * *

STARS AND STRIPES

1. Transatlantic Runaround

Last week in Paris
Next week in Spain
No sooner do you get home
Than you're off again

Crossing the Atlantic
Just for the day
Wherever there is action
You are on the way

Transatlantic runaround
Get your feet back on the ground
Better slow down the pace
Or you won't finish the race

Jet-setting baby
Looking for the light
But when the party's over
Tears fill your night

...ve is waiting for you
If you'll look and see
You can leave the treadmill
And be really free

Transatlantic runaround
Get your feet back on the ground
Better slow down the pace
Or you won't finish the race

2. Airport
Hundreds of people
Running around
Business as usual
So much sound

Cases and tickets
An early flight
If it goes well
They'll be home tonight

And in the crowd you're lonely
Noise is all around you
In the midst of all the people
Does anyone love you?

Fly to the sunshine
Have a winter break
But there's no answer
To that longing ache

A crowd of strangers
All on their own
Smiling politely
Feeling alone

And in the crowd you're lonely
Noise is all around you
In the midst of all the people
Does anyone love you?

Somebody loves you
His favourite word is 'come'
Take that final flight
And you will be home.

3. Future Fright
Walking down memory lane
Trying to avoid the pain

Got to fade away
Back into yesterday
Hearing familiar sounds
Living on safe ground
You're happy here
Hope that it won't disappear

Anything that keeps you young
You will spend your money on
Living fast and free
It's the only way to be
Don't want to hear about tomorrow
Walking backwards from the edge
    of sorrow
You'd rather be blind
Shut it out of your mind

The day is almost over
And soon will come the night
If you look you'll see an answer
To your future fright

You can't run forever
Living on the never-never
Enjoying what is past
Hoping it will last
Tomorrow may be full of doubt
But it can all work out
No need for you to cry
Take a step - go on - try.

The day is almost over
And soon will come the night
If you look you'll see an answer
To your future fright

Though your mind's full of fear
There is something who can hear
The questions in your brain
And is ready to explain
The time has come to make a move
From a world of hate to love
He will lead you on
The past is dead and gone

The day is almost over
And soon will come the night
If you look you'll see an answer
To your future fright

4. First Lady (of Washington)

It was so good to see you
I could see that you were alright
That you were really happy
Soaking up the sunlight

Caught you by surprise
Hope you didn't mind
It was just a joke
Wasn't meant to be unkind

Hey, how are you
After all this time
It's good to know
That you are doing fine

We talked of many things
And of close friends too
And I enjoyed every minute
Hope you did too
Hey, how are you
After all this time
It's good to know
That you are doing fine

After I left you
Got soaked in the rain
So goodbye
Until we meet again

Hey, how are you
After all this time
It's good to know
That you are doing fine

5. Voices in the crowd

Listen to him speaking
See his need
A hungry man
Whom you forgot to feed

A man of sorrow
See him cry
Talking to himself
While you pass by

And you believe in free speech
If it's not too loud
Your ears are closed
To the voices in the crowd

He brings good news
But you won't hear
Don't want to change
Too much fear

And you believe in free speech
If it's not too loud
Your ears are closed
To the voices in the crowd

The day will come
In the midst of the violence
Then all you'll hear
Is the roar of silence

And you believe in free speech
If it's not too loud
Your ears are closed
To the voices in the crowd

6. Cruising

The radio is playing
And the music is so good
And my heart is singing
Just like it should
DC 101 is rocking
And the sun is shining bright
And if we keep this speed up
We'll be in Washington tonight

Cruising in the warmth of your love
Travelling down the 95
Hey, Lord, you're so good to me
And it's so good to be alive

Met a lot of people
Who were really kind
Yeh, those kind of people
Blow my mind
We had our troubles
But you were always there
And even back home
I'll never forget your care
Cruising in the warmth of your love

Travelling down the 95
Hey, Lord, you're so good to me
And it's so good to be alive

7. Whatever Happened To The All-American Dream

This land was a great land
For the strong and free
Where a man could grow
To be what he should be
A home for all nations
Good things to share
Where you could be certain
That the verdict was just and fair

Now there's an emptiness within her
And it makes her want to scream
Whatever happened
To the all-American dream?

It used to be a strong land
'In God we trust;'
Now its hopes and morals
Are crumbled in the dust
There's so much disillusion
And the future brings only fear
And the time of no return
Is drawing near

Now there's an emptiness within
her
And it makes her want to scream
Whatever happened
To the all-American dream?

* * *

DELUDED

Oh, my friend, can't you see, your life is slipping away
You think you have everything, but it's starting to decay
And when your life is through, what will you have won?
You'll be left in the darkness when the race is done

If you think you have everything, then it's all in your head
But when it comes to reality, you'll find that you're deluded

You've spent a lot of time on things that don't last
Money, parties and pleasures, they disappear so fast
Now I'm not saying that you shouldn't have joy
But there has to be a reckoning, it comes nearer every day

If you think you have everything, then it's all in your head
But when it comes to reality, you'll find that you're deluded

You looked for reality and values that were true
But when you saw how much it would cost, it wasn't for you
And so you waste your time, living for today
Tomorrow doesn't matter - it's too far away

If you think you have everything, then it's all in your head
But when it comes to reality, you'll find that you're deluded

And when the time comes round to look at your life
What will you have to show - only hate, pain and strife
You think that you are happy, that you've got it worked out
But when the darkness closes around you, you begin to doubt

If you think you have everything, then it's all in your head
But when it comes to reality, you'll find that you're deluded

Now if you're not satisfied with the life you lead
There's someone who can help you from the chains you'll be freed
He's been there all the time, while you followed your mind
Truth, love, peace, are what he gives, turn around and you'll find!

If you think you have everything, then it's all in your head
But when it comes to reality, you'll find that you're deluded

* * *

NAZARETH AGAIN

I came to you with a heart full of peace
A message of hope that will make your pain cease
But you wouldn't listen, you turned me away
And told me to come back some other day

> And standing in darkness
> You can't see my pain
> I'm feeling just like Jesus
> It's Nazareth again

Your eyes were filled with laughter, mocking and scorn
When I said the night was over and soon there'd be dawn
And you thought you'd be alright and that you could cope
And it hurts me to see you resting on false hope

> And standing in darkness
> You can't see my pain
> I'm feeling just like Jesus
> It's Nazareth again

Perhaps one day I'll be able to return
And your ears will be open ready to learn
Believe that I love you but I have to go
For there are many waiting and the truth they want to know

> And standing in darkness
> You can't see my pain
> I'm feeling just like Jesus
> It's Nazareth again

* * *

CROSSROADS

> I started out so long ago
> On the journey of my life
> Through the traffic of confusion
> On the motorway of strife
> Will I reach my destination

Find the peace I'm looking for
Reaching ever closing door?

And I'm standing at the crossroads
Wondering which is the way
And the moon is shining brightly
At the end of another day

I thought that you'd be happy
Always looking for the sun
Spending nights in joy and pleasure
Always looking for some fun
But the time moves on so quickly
And I'm getting near the end
I've never really settled
And I've never had a friend
And I'm standing at the crossroads
Wondering which is the way
And the moon is shining brightly
At the end of another day

Now the choice is there before me
And I don't know what to do
There are so many options open
But only one is true
Is there someone who could help me
And show me what is right
I'm standing in the darkness
And I need to find the light

And I'm standing at the crossroads
Wondering which is the way
And the moon is shining brightly
At the end of another day

FOUR MINUTES AND COUNTING
Never thought it would come to this
This is a day I hoped I'd miss
Oh, what a day
Got to get away!
The news has come like a bombshell
And as far as I can tell
There's no escape
It's much too late

Four minutes and counting
We had so long to decide
Now the time has all run out
And there's nowhere left to hide

Now the future has come round
Creeping up without a sound
It's such a crime
All that wasted time
The warning signs were plain to see
But we said it could never be
Now it's here -
We're in the grip of fear

Four minutes and counting
We had so long to decide
Now the time has all run out
And there's nowhere left to hide

* * *

SHED YOUR GENTLE LOVE

Shed your gentle love on me
And lift me when I'm down
You have the power to change me
So I may wear a crown
Take my heart, it's yours now
I want to be like you
I'm waiting now, shed your love on me

So often I have let you down
When I could have done more
Now I'm begging on my knees
Please don't shut the door
I long to give you glory
To walk closer to you
I'm waiting now, shed your love on me

Please won't you help me
I need your gentle hand
I want to walk beside you
In the life that you have planned

Take me as you find me
I won't hide from you
I long to be surrounded
By your love which is so true
I'll give you everything, my Lord
If you will set me free
I'm waiting now, shed your love on me

* * *

ARMAGEDDON'S CALLING

I heard the news today
Troops are on the way
Just another power play
With different names

Another crisis here -
We have lost count this year
While East and West
Play the same old games

And the peace that we're looking for
Is rapidly disappearing
Listen! You can hear it on the wind
Armageddon's calling

New weapons build security
Preserve the life of the free
It's good for you
For you have no choice

And those who disagree aren't heard
Love's treated like a dirty word
Might is right
No time for a quiet voice

And the peace that we're looking for
Is rapidly disappearing
Listen! You can hear it on the wind
Armageddon's calling

The precipice is close at hand
But mocked are those who understand
But in the tragic final hour
We'll see who holds the real power.

The One who's held it from the beginning

* * *

JESUS

In the midst of darkness
He is the Light
And every wrong there is
He will put right

First time in humility
Sweat upon his brow
Some just would not listen
It's a different story now

Jesus -
There'll be an end to all the pain
And there will be peace
When he comes again

Jesus -
There'll be an end to all the pain
And there will be peace
When he comes again

Hear the sound of rustling leaves
See the shining moon
Time is ticking quietly away
He is coming soon

Soon the years of waiting
Will end in liberty
And all will see him reigning
In glorious majesty

Jesus -
There'll be an end to all the pain
And there will be peace
When he comes again

Jesus -
There'll be an end to all the pain
And there will be peace
When he comes again

* * *

Chapter 4
Freedom Song (1985)

Alyn says: A time of frustration, it is very hard when God calls you and nobody realises it. It was a time of travel to Denmark and the USA for Olympic effort, but also a time of trouble as I lost money trying to get this book published. Cheated by crooks.

ALYN HASKEY

Alyn was born in 1951 and due to an accident has Cerebral Palsy. His early life was a constant struggle against frustration, coupled with difficulties in communication, which resulted in an assessment that education for him would be a waste of time.

At the age of 14, Alyn found Jesus, and, in his words, it changed his life. From that time he has taken 'A levels, a BA Hons degree from York, a Licentiate in Theology from St John's in Nottingham and has recently gained a BA from the Open University. He has also got Duke of Edinburgh bronze, silver and gold awards and has represented England and Great Britain in international sport, gaining bronze medals.

Since 1981, he has exercised an itinerant evangelistic and teaching ministry, travelling extensively in Britain and America, and is available to come and speak, or share poetry and music

In this fourth book he shares once again his faith, in a selection of poems addressing issues which face the world, and the answer to those questions

OCTOBER IN ENGLAND

October in England
Early morning rain
Summer seems so distant
Winter comes again;
Fog swirling round
Covering the ground,
There's an aching inside me
Will I see the sun again?

October in England
The leaves are fading fast,
Sun gives way to wind
Days of gold are quickly past,
Frosty hands reach out
And in my heart there's doubt
An emptiness inside me
Tell me, who can ease the pain?

Another year is ending
And with the wind I"m bending
But will I break
Or stand firm?

October in England
And soon the winter will be here,
But if you are here beside me
There's no fear
For your love will keep me true and
      strong
Although the winter's long
And I will come to no harm
For in the storm you are the calm

* * *

A LOVE LIKE YOURS

I wake up in the morning
Hoping for another good day,
But sometimes my expectations
Seem to go astray

I know I'm not perfect
I don't do all I should,
But I know you won't turn your back
When it's hard to be good

And I don't understand
Why you've chosen me,
But with a love like yours
I know I can be free

Sometimes I let you down
And I feel full of shame
But when I turn to face you
I see you love me just the same

You're the greatest thing in my life,
Without you I couldn't cope,
When the storm-clouds gather
You turn despair into hope

Your love is so amazing
It takes away my pain,
It's a love that goes on and on
Surprising me again and again

* * *

BLOOD ON THE TRACK

Tears of pain
Flowing down
Blood they spattered
On the ground

Another victim,
Another headline,
Gun and bullet,
Bomb and mine

Israel, Poland,
Ireland, Rome,
Yet always somewhere
They find a home

Might is right
So join the fight
Don't contemplate
Death or blight

Yet there is something
You should know,
There is a limit
How far can you go

Killing for Jesus
Your excuse a lie
He came to give us life
Not to die

Soon there'll be
No turning hack,
The record is made,
There's blood on the track

THE CLOWN

The crowds have all gone home,
In the ring he stands alone,
His tricks have brought much laughter,
Sad feelings always come after

He is the clown
Who wears a comic crown,
But no-one sees inside
When he tries to hide.

* * *

WHEN I WAS YOUNG

When I was young
Everything was magic,
The world was beautiful,
Life was good,
Plenty to look forward to,
But now, it's all gone sour

When I was young
Jobs were plenty,
Engine-driver, policeman, soldier,
Prospects were good
But now the dole queues stretch for miles

When I was young
I believed in Santa Claus,
In happy endings,
Everything coming right,
'Happily-ever-after';
But now all I see around is heartbreak and sadness.

When I was young
The war was over,
Everyone was at peace,
We were all friends again
Living together in harmony,
But now at any moment, the Bomb could drop

When I was young
I heard about Jesus
- that he died to make me good
- that I had plenty of time to make him my friend
- there's no rush to be saved

But now?

OH WHAT A YEAR

I've seen all my hopes
Crumble just like sand,
Dreams have just disappeared
Everything we've planned
But though I cannot see.
I know you've got the best for me
And time is in your hand
Now I understand.

Oh what a year it's been
Can't explain the things I've seen
But I know I'm in your care.
Oh what a year.

The future's uncertain
Where will I go?
Every time I find the answer
You say 'no'
But of one thing I am sure
You hold the keys to the door
And I know your love is true
So I'll trust you.

And if it takes forever
I will not mind
For I know you are guiding me
Without you, I'm blind

* * *

JERUSALEM, JERUSALEM

Jerusalem, Jerusalem,
The city waits for him
And loud hosannas cry
'Here comes your king'
But all too soon you change

Jerusalem, Jerusalem
At dead of night they creep
And in the garden
The pain is there to see
A prisoner taken in chains

Jerusalem, Jerusalem
A silent hill greets the dawn
And on a cross he hangs on high
Soon he will die
And the earth will shake

Jerusalem, Jerusalem
The day has come
The stone has rolled from the
        empty tomb
And he is standing in the upper room
Jesus is alive

Jerusalem, Jerusalem
You wait in hope and pain
But your King will come again
And he will break the chain
And for evermore will reign.

FIVE MINUTES TO MIDNIGHT

I woke up this morning
Another dreary day,
Somebody told me
War is on the way
Who has the answer
Where can we turn?
Or will we be caught up
In the final burn?

Five minutes to midnight
Who knows where we're going?
How much time do we have left?
Must we reap what we're sowing?

Politicians tell us
The future's bright,
We're at the end of the tunnel
Walking in the light
But millions are starving
On television to view
And all the optimism
Seems so untrue

Crises come so quickly
What happened to peace?
Every day new tragedies
When will it cease?
But in the midst of darkness
There's a soft still voice
His hands are scarred and bleeding
But only we have the choice.

* * *

COMING

When he comes again
He will bring the sound of laughter?
And the earth will sing with joy
The songs of old

When He comes again
We will see His shining glory
And the shackles will be broken
We'll be free

He will put an end to pain and sorrow,
He will bring new hope for tomorrow.
He will reign for ever
The King of kings
And Lord of lords, Amen

When He comes again
To the sound of Hallelujah,
The night will be destroyed
And day will come

He will put an end to pain and sorrow
He will bring new hope for tomorrow,
He will reign for ever,
The King of kings
And Lord of lords. Amen

* * *

HOT LINE

Chilly winds blowing all around me
It's night time in the city
Everyone's a stranger
And there ain't no pity
I need some help tonight

I need a hot-line
To help me survive
I don't feel fine
Can't see me staying alive
Hot-line, is there someone who loves me?

I look for love in every face
But it just isn't there
I need someone who understands
Is there anyone to care?
I need some help tonight

And I know my life ain't so good
And I would change it if only I could

There must be someone I can turn to
Who can turn a wrong to right
I'd give him everything I have
If he'd turn my darkness into light
I need some help tonight

I need a hot-line
To help me survive
I don't feel fine
Can't see me staying alive
Hot-line, is there someone who loves me?

* * *

SUPER-HEROES

Get on the hot-line straight away
We need help tonight
We need the caped crusader,
We're in a terrible plight
Call down Superman
From the sky
we're getting desperate,
Will we live or die?

Everybody needs a Super hero
To make the story come out right,
But the man who died upon a cross
Is the one who's won the fight.

Wonder Woman is on the case
She'll have it cracked,
Spiderman can spin a web
And have the villains trapped
Call In the FBI
And CIA
R2, D2 and C3PO
Will win the day.

We all want liberty,
And war to cease
But somehow the people we call on
Don't bring us peace
But there's a man called Jesus
Who died on a cross,
Who gives us life abundantly,
And turns the bad to good

* * *

THE TURNING POINT.

All my hopes lay broken
Scattered on the ground,
The hopeful dreams of yesterday
Were nowhere to be found

The loneliness around me
Was too much to bear
In my anguish I cried out
'Is there anyone to care?'

I've gone as far as I can go
I don't feel I'll survive,
But I have reached the turning point
And now I see that you're alive

It's so hard to understand
Why these things should be
But there's a point to all the sorrow
When we begin to see

From tragedy comes triumph
And joy comes out of pain
For my hopes rise in the morning light
With you I live again

I've gone as far as I can go
I don't feel I'll survive,
But I have reached the turning point
And now I see that you're alive

* * *

JUST AS I AM.

I would have done anything you wanted
But I'm useless at everything
And all my attempts to impress you
Have that hollow ring.

Just as I am,
That's how you want me
You open my eyes to see,
Just as I are
Without pretending
Your love has set me free.

In my own strength I can do nothing,
It doesn't matter what I do
All I can do is surrender
And leave it up to you

It doesn't matter what others think,
When I am weak then you are strong.
I know my performance is shaky
I know that you're the song.

* * *

ANY MORE

War is sin,
Sin is war,
Got to stop the fighting,
Won't take any more

We've got to live together
In perfect harmony,
Break the chains of bondage
So we'll all be free.

We're all brothers and sisters
It's time to care,
We have a beautiful world
Which we should share.

War is sin,
Sin is war
Get to step the fighting,
Won't take any more.

Let the children of God
Bring Jesus' peace,
Put an end to hostility,
Then war will cease.

Time is running out,
This is the day,
Hear the word of Jesus,
He is the way.

War is sin.
Sin is war,
Got to stop the fighting,
Won't take any more.

* * *

FREEDOM SONG.

I heard a distant thunder
As the earth began to shake,
A sound of revolution in the air
The sky began to darken
And the sea began to roar
For the time of revelation is here

Repression's hand was bleeding
And fear had run away,
And the gates of death lay broken on the ground
And the prison of oppression
Its walls began to crack
As the final trumpet blasted out its sound

And we shall rise like the sun
And it will not be too long,
For no-one can stop us
Sing our freedom song

At the breaking of the morning
We stand ready to move,
For there are those still fastened in chains
But the enemies of love
Are fleeing hour by hour
As they see the face of Him who ends all pain.

For He is risen
And the grave has lost its power,
And we are waiting in the wings
For His triumphant hour
And I was once a prisoner
In selfish agony
Heading for the dark world of night.,
And then He broke my bondage
My eyes began to see,
And now I live in freedom"s golden light

And you, will you be taken
The dungeon yawning wide
Captivity for all eternity?
Dr will you turn to Jesus
And join our victory march?
Come and sing the song of the free

And we shall rise like the sun
And it will not be to long
For no-one can stop us
Sing our freedom song

AMERICA THE BEAUTIFUL.

Good morning, America,
Let's see what's going on
All your hopes and aspirations
With the wind have gone
Violence on the corners
Prostitution there to see,
You get all your opinions
From the man who's on TV

America the beautiful
The castle's falling down,
You used to rule the world
And now you've lost your crown.

You don't know what you're doing
Trapped by indecision,
The unity we look for
Is crushed by your division
Your weapons of security
Send millions to their graves
And you don't hear the message
That only Jesus saves

You put your trust in freezers
And anything that will sell,
You're looking hard for Paradise
But all you find is Hell
And yet He still loves you
To you that might seem odd,
So why not turn and face Him
Renew your trust in God

QUEEN OF THE SPACE-INVADERS

Every night she makes her way
To the magic machine,
Fame at her finger tips,
Top of the scene

She's the queen of the
space-invaders
She's get the highest score.
And as long as they keep landing
She'll go on for evermore.

Her hands are on the buttons,
Ready, steady, go
She's got it all worked out
There's nothing she needs to know.

But the night is quickly over,
Reluctantly she goes home
Wishing it could last for ever
Hating to be alone.

There'll come a time when the lights will fade
And the game will come to an end
Machines can never return the love
That comes from a true friend.

* * *

FOUR SEASONS

DARK DAYS OF WINTER.
In the dark days of winter
Wind is blowing strong,
Days are very short,
Nights are very long

Winter sun
Hardly ever seen,
Every tree and blade
A dirty shade of green

Will the spring come?
Will life begin again?

RISING SPRING
Awaken with the dawn,
Life is born again,
The birds are singing sweetly
Angel choirs sing
The Lord of life is risen
Empty stands the tomb,
The sun brings forth its promise
Clouds no longer hide the moon

So run with the Son
For He has risen
And we shall never die again.

HOT SUMMER
Hot summer
Down on the beach

Distant dreams
Come within reach.

Shining water
Bright and clear,
Invitingly welcome
No need to fear
Long summer nights
Full of fun,
Days of warmth
Lying in the sun.

It's good to be alive,
To enjoy what's here
A summer break.
The high spot of the year.

AUTUMN EMBERS
Leaves turn brown
Drawing from the trees
Ankle deep, waist deep
Far above our knees

The sun feels colder,
Time is moving on
The last breeze of summer
Will soon be gone

Memories we treasure
Photographs on card.
New winter beckons,
Hope it's not too hard

I see winter round me
Wrapped up to keep warm,
Uneasy peace and stillness
Before the raging storm

But soon it will be Christmas.

* * *

MORNING

Jerusalem
They saw Him come
With palms and branches
Made Him welcome
But soon the shouts
They turned to hate
As He moved on
It was His fate

In secret meet
For His defeat
The plot was made
To bring Him down
At night betrayed
His friends afraid
Whipped and scourged
And thorny crowned

When daylight came
In tears of shame
And these who falsely
Told a lie
To Calvary
On wooden tree
There they mocked
And left to die

For six long hours
Tortured by pain
Till earth did shake
And all was gloom,
Oh it is finished.'
He did cry
Thou laid Him down
In a stranger's tomb.

As morning broke
And rose the sun
Then opened wide
Was that great door
And from the grave
All men to save
He rose to life
To die no more

AT THE COMING OF THE MAN
The sun is fading
The stars fall from the sky
And the world you know makes no
                    sense at all
And the nations struggle
And when they reach the top
There seems no time before they
                    start to fall

What about tomorrow?
Will it ever come?
Can we hope to see the light of day?
For the time has come
As He prophesied
For all things must pass away.

And you say you can't believe it
But where will you run,
At the coming of the Man
And the burning of the sun?

There will be a sound
And lightning from the east
But then everything will be made clear
And on that day
The old will pass away
No more pain, death and fear
                    * * *

GUITAR
Guitar I see you standing there
Strings taut
Melody waiting to burst forth,
Songs of joy straining to be heard
One day I will play you
                    * * *

THE DREAM
Laughed at,
Stared at,
Avoided and feared,

Unusual,
Astounding,
To be shunned as weird

A painful encounter
A churning inside
Hurried conversation
Then run away and hide

Silently wondering who is to blame
Funny when Jesus can accept me
                    as I am

One day my dream will come true
Then you'll see that I'm really just
                    like you
                    * * *

1981 (FALSE DAWN)
For a minute, I was almost a person
Almost real
Me before wheel
In the public eye
People showed concern
Wanted to help
To accept me as an equal
To give me a place in society
But then the clock struck midnight
                    * * *

UNDESIRABLE ALIEN

We don't want to hear you talk
We're happy as we are
We don't want to see you around
You should be put behind bars

The sight of you makes us sick
They should put you away
When you came into town
That was a terrible day

Undesirable alien
Why don't you go home?
There is no place for you
Go back where you came from

We were perfectly happy
'Til you came on the scene
Your message offends our ears
Go before we get mean

Your way of life is stupid
The world is for the strong
And if you continue in what you do
You won't live long

Undesirable alien
Why don't you go home?
There is no place for you
Go back where you came from

And so they nailed him to a cross
And they thought that he was gone
But his life could not be ended
And his message goes on and on

Undesirable alien
Why don't you go home?
There is no place for you
Go back where you came from
* * *

STAR WARS

Three, two, one, BLAST OFF!
A hundred miles in space
They've got a super weapon
To annihilate the human race

Star wars
We can blow ourselves to pieces
But no-ones got an answer
To ensure that all war ceases

Radar stations monitor
Every move we make
And we are held in terror
In case there's a simple mistake

Man will rule the universe
That's what the propagandists say
But there's another Super-power
And soon we'll see his day
* * *

CHRISTMAS

Snow is falling all around
Carols hum their sweet sad sound
Lights in shops shine bright and clear
Soon the great day will be here
A time of hope
Goodwill and peace
And many blessings
That never cease
Sentimental songs
Are sung
Soon the Christmas bells
Are rung
For some, joy cannot be seen
The homeless, lonely, misshaped,
            unclean -
Only fears for them this year
And next, another, filled with fear
And He who came
A babe - so poor
Still waits outside
Every locked door
To every heart
Continues to come
And asks,
'Have you any room?'
* * *

FEBRUARY

Snow-covered memories
Hidden from sight
Cold wind blowing
Long dark night

Hopes lie frozen
Dreams are gone
Already it seems
Winter's been too long

Frustration and fears
Sadness and pain
I begin to wonder
Will the sun shine again?

And yet I know
The sun will break through the haze
And put an end
To February days

* * *

AFTER ALL THIS TIME (COMMUNION).

We've come a long way together
And at times it's been rough
But when I'm feeling tired
Your love is always enough

We've had many adventures
And we've been close to the edge
But when I was slipping
You put my foot back on the ledge

There's nothing on earth
Could make me change my mind
I could never leave you
After all this time

Sometimes we have disagreements
And maybe I want to shout
But when I stop and listen to you
You take away my doubt

There's nothing I like better
Than to be alone with you
My life is yours forever
Because I know your love is true

Draw me close to your side
That's where I always want to be
We'll share a life together
In sweet communion we can be free

* * *

MAGIC

I am the sorcerer
The man of mystery
It's the soul that I want
You can never be free
I will work such wonders
No tongue could ever tell
Strange and mysterious signs
As you journey into Hell

My name is Magic
Quickness of the hand deceives
I am destruction
For anyone who believes

The gates of Babylon
Beckon to you
But leave behind
All which is true
Pleasures and ecstasies
A world of night
When daybreak brings the reckoning
I'll be nowhere in sight

And when your heart is mine
And you're wrapped up in my chain
Then false dreams you'll discover
And all will turn to pain
My work will be over
And captive will you be
For my time is running out
And you will die with me

* * *

ON THE STREET

Looking for action,
Looking for fun,
Joy is a mirage
Always on the run
Left home
To find some peace
But these troubles
Never cease

It doesn't matter how you feel
It's the only place to be real,
Like-minded people you will meet
On the street

City lights shining
But they start to fade
Look at my life
What a mess I've made
Is there someone
Who can lend me a hand
Answer the questions
I don't understand?

Time is running out
I can't wait
No turning back
It could be too late
Maybe Jesus
Will hear me cry
Help me Lord
Before I die

* * *

CRYSTAL TEARS (OF ETERNITY)
I'm on my own again
My heart is full of pain
And where have all my dreams gone?

I could smile yesterday
But the sun's gone away
And I wonder for how long

But I know He loves me
I have no need to fear
And I'm crying now
He will make it right
Because He keeps every crystal tear

* * *

GREY SKIES WILL
TURN TO BLUE.
It may be raining
But I know it won't last long,
And when I'm feeling down
You know what's wrong

There are so many things
I just don't understand,
But when the doubts come round
You hold me in your hand

Even when the rain pours down
I know it's true
In just a little while
Grey skies will turn to blue

I need your love
Every single day
And the greatest joy
Is to hear the words you say

So let the rain come down,
I will not despair
I have the certainty
You will always be there

Even when the rain pours down
I know it's true
In just a little while
Grey skies will turn to blue

* * *

ANGEL WITH A DIRTY FACE.
My jeans are patched and torn,
My face looks haggard and worn
My hair is long;
And my fashion is way behind in time
But though I look a mess
You can see I'm happy, I guess
Whether it rains or shines
I'll be feeling fine

Well, I'm an angel with a dirty face
And I'm lagging behind in the race,
But Jesus love is gonna
Help me make it through

I like my rock 'n' roll loud
And I like being one of the crowd;
And when the guitar's playing
I want to dance and sing
But I know who saved my soul,
And I know who makes me whole,
And I will praise His name
Because Jesus is my King

Some people think I'm crazy,
Others say I'm lazy;
But Jesus sees
The truth is written in my heart
I'm gonna follow Him for ever
Where He wants to lead
Because when I was down and out
He was the one who gave me a new
start

* * *

IN EVERYTHING GIVE THANKS
(A SONG FOR JONI)

When the road is steep and rocky,
When the journey seems so long,
Then I know that you're beside me
For you fill my heart with song

And if the sun is shining,
Or if the rain is pouring down,
With Jesus there beside me
I can face whatever comes
For His love gives me the strength to say
In everything give thanks

There are times when I am happy
And everything is fine
But even when the sky's grey
You are with me all the time

I have no fears for tomorrow
With Jesus as my friend,
And one day I'll see Him face to face
At my journey's end

Chapter 5
Prodigal World (1986)

Alyn Says: Hope springs eternal and at last the barriers begin to come down. Finally people begin to recognise that God has called you and doors begin to open.

FOREWORD

Here is a new collection of poems that spotlight some of the issues we are faced with, living in the world today, but they are also about an endless love which, if we will receive it, can give us all we need to live in peace.

Alyn is a poet and song writer, who, though born with a severe disability, has experienced many miracles through his faith in Jesus, including degrees in History, Theology, and Social Sciences, plus international selection in sport for England and Great Britain.

He is now a commended evangelist, and travels widely, but is always open to invitations to minister

THE NIGHT

The sky grows darker
The rain will come
Trapped in the shadowland
So far from home.

My enemies gather
To watch me fall
But I know my shepherd
Will hear my call.

In the valley of shadow
I will walk by your light
And the darkness will flee
No fear in the night

With all my doubts
Surrounded by fear and pain
Your love will touch me
And restore me again

On the journey
You will lead and guide
And when in danger
In You I will hide

In your presence
I will rest and stay
And see all afflictions
Vanish on that day

* * *

CHRISTMAS IS COMING

Christmas is coming
Soon we'll all be fat,
A penny for the poor
The rest for your new hat!
King's carols on the radio
War on the telly
Fears about peace talks,
Mixed with cream and jelly.

Jesus in a cow shed
Shivering from the cold
Children facing danger
No chance to grow old;
It's just what I wanted
Think how much we'll save!
The shops are open Tuesday
We'll swap the gift that Jesus gave

* * *

SEPTEMBER

Back home again
Been a long time
But it's been good
To see what you can do

Summer's gone
Autumn winds
Busy days
Are nearly through

September here again
You promised much
But seemed to disappear
Remember in the midst of pain
His love endures
And He is always near

All the hopes
And dreams crash down
And every day
Brings problems to the fore

But now you've ended
Though the problems hang on
When I am weak
Your strength is seen much more

As the days go by
I may cry
But your hand is reaching
Out to me

And the time will come
When the pain will end
And your victory
I will clearly see

* * *

DODGEM

Chorus:
Jesus on the dodgems
Driving so fast
I've got to get out of the way
Revving up the engine
Taking off the brake
Don't want to hear what He's got to say

Verse I
Always been an easy rider
Fastest on the track
In top gear all the way
Then I saw this car approaching
Couldn't match His power
Now it seems I've had my day

Verse 2
Weaving in and out of traffic
Try to hide away
But every time I look He's still there
I thought I was the king
Every road was mine
But now my mind is full of fear

Verse 3
Can I drive this car forever?
Driving round in circles
Not really knowing where to go
Or should I cut the engine
Let Him have the lead
Because I'll always be too slow

* * *

SATURDAY
NEW YORK IN THE RAIN

Radios playing a gentle song
WLTW travelling along
Lazy Saturday
A chance to get away

Think about the things you said
See your face inside my head
Memories to see
Laughter is a joy to me

The distance so far
Will we meet again?
Thinking about you
Saturday! New York in the rain

Didn't see much from the tower
Never had so short an hour
Time to go
Journey back long and slow

Someday may return again
To share New York in the rain
Of all the things we talked of
Hope that you find Jesus' love

* * *

'A LETTER TO SANTA'

What do you want for Christmas?
When Santa comes to call
Write your dreams in a letter
Maybe you'll get them all
A stereo hi-fi centre
A walking, crying doll
A supa dupa video
A real leather football
The top five records
A bicycle to ride
Beer and fags for Dad

For Mum a handbag of real hide
What would you like for Christmas
Little child so thin and small?
With a voice so soft and gentle
Who is never heard at all
A crust of bread and water
An end to pain and fear
A promise from all governments
That we'll be here next year.

* * *

GIRL IN A MOVIE
Your life is just beginning
And hopes are very high
Just a little accident
There's more than meets the eye

Fears and hopes are mingled
The answer no-one can guess
A minor operation
It could be a success

Picking up the threads
But the news isn' t good
Now the questions rise
How can it be understood?

Life runs quickly away
But soon there'll be release
Now you face eternity
Hoping for real peace

Girl in a movie
For you it's nearly through
But for many others
This reality is true

* * *

DON'T FEED THE ANIMALS
Early morning, cold weather
Travelling on a train
Sorry, no facilities
Guard's van again
Cage is shut, people walk.
Things I have to bear
Trying to avert their eyes
Still they stand and stare
Back and forth they pass
Looking left and right;
Please don't feed the animals
Or one day they might bite

HOUSE OF SAND
A good life is exciting
And pleasure is your aim
And no-one can criticise
Or give you the blame
But life is more than riches
And video games
And if it all vanished
Would you feel the same?

You want the best of both worlds
That I can understand
But when the wind blows
And the water flows
What will happen
To your house of sand?

Parties bring you pleasure
You love the social scene
And every new fashion
Finds you there so keen
But time will take its toll
And age is always mean
And when the grey hairs show
Will you still want to be seen?

Dreams are ten a penny
You can throw them away
And when it comes to words of
                    wisdom
You don't hear a word I say
But when the sand runs out
And you need someone to care
Then maybe you'll realise
That he's always been there

And those who build their house on
                    sand
They cannot understand
That only Jesus
Has the key
And only He
Can set you free

* * *

HI THERE!
Hi there!
Must dash!
Got to rush
Nice to see you

Like to talk
But I......
You know how it is!
Yes, I'll talk to you
Sometime.....
Bye!
* * *

STOP THE WORLD I WANT TO GET ON

People running everywhere
Trying to make sense of it all
I wait in my small corner
Hoping that someone will call

They're all trying to escape
Got their eyes on the stars above
Stop the world I want to get on
I've been touched by His love

No-one seems to notice me
What in the world could I do
But I've got a secret to tell you
I've found a love which is true

You don't have to go round in circles
Just stop and look at His face
He has solutions to our problems
He paid the price for the whole
                              universe

You can keep chasing shadows
Live your life believing it's unreal
Or you can give Him your pains
                              and scars
His healing hand you will feel

Don't let the world pull you down
Don't believe the old familiar story
We're not destined to live second class
He intends that we share His glory!
* * *

SHADOWS

Shadows falling on the hill
Darkest secrets bend my will
Fear, oppression
Doubt cascading
Wishing to be free

Another shadow on the hill
A wooden cross
Nails in deep
Victim hanging
In death he sleeps.
Early morning
Shadows in a cave
Jesus risen
For us to save
Shadows flee
And we are free
* * *

THE CLUB

I was going to be a human
But they wouldn't let me in
They said I was a fire risk
My brain was much too thin

They couldn't get me up the steps
So they locked the door
Suggested that a Country Club
Would probably suit me more

But as I rolled back down the hill
Floating in my tears
I noticed Jesus was coming too
He's been trying to get in for years
* * *

CITY

Bright lights shine
Reflected in the street
Somewhere the music's playing
Can't you hear the beat?

Cold wind blowing
Fear in every face
Searching in the ruins
For a hiding place

People walk through the centre
But in their eyes there's no pity
Where is love for those who cry?
Lost in the city

The bells ring out
A new day dawns
Wrapped in his newspaper
A lonely stranger yawns

Violence calls out
Another night of fear
And those who should be listening
Don't really want to hear

Voices on the radio
Another lame excuse
We'd like to help
But it's just no use

And he's standing in the gutter
In the darkened alley he is there
And he stretches out his nailed,
scarred hands
The marks of his love and care

And people still keep walking
And some may show a little pity
And Jesus stands with those who cry
Love has come to the city

* * *

TWILIGHT ZONE
You're walking in darkness
Fears grip your heart
Shadows are moving
See their eyes dart

You wish there were someone
Who could hold your hand
And when you have anxious feelings
They would understand

The day is fading fast
But you're not on your own
Jesus is with you
In the twilight zone

Your mind is confusion
And you long for peace
He has the answers
To make your nightmares cease

* * *

RUNNING FOR THE PRIZE
On and on I go
Looking straight ahead
Energy disappearing
Feeling almost dead

Another circuit over
Twenty more to go
It's hard to raise the pace
Faster than dead slow

When the rain is pouring
Or the sun is shining bright
Gusting winds carry you
Almost out of sight

A trip, a slip, disaster!
Grimacing with pain
Wheels stiff, immovable
Needing oil again!

But time is ticking away
And now I'm feeling fine
The race is nearly over
There's the finishing line!

As long as I can look up
And see Jesus before my eyes
No matter how many obstacles
I'll keep running for the prize

* * *

PRODIGAL
Part 1
Trapped in a cage longing to get out
Searching for freedom,
cannot you hear me shout.
A life of excitement
A life of fun
Where the music plays all night
Days of warmth and sun
Please don't try to hold me
I've got to go.
When I return
I do not know

Far Country Calling
Far country calling to me
Don't you know I want to be free,
I've been stuck round here
For so many years
How I want to see what life is like
Please let me go
There's so much I want to know
I want to go where the lights
always shine

You always tell me to wait
But it's getting late
I want to go before my time is gone
Yes, I know that you care
But please give me my share
Darkness comes, another day is gone
I know you'll miss me
But I've just got to go
I'll come back soon
So don't worry

Part 2
The city light shines
Now is the right time
This is what I want

Exciting sights
Long nights
This is what I want

New found friends
I hope it never ends
This is what I want

In the City

In the city tonight
It's gonna be alright
I've got money in my pocket
Let the good times roll
I've got lots of friends
I hope it never ends
The music is so good
It really speaks to my soul

In the city, in the city
I'm gonna have some fun
Dance and sing all night long
And sleep all day in the sun

You know the living is good
I'd make it last if I could
But the money's getting low
And friends are starting to go
I'm getting short of everything
I'll have to sell my ring
I've got to get a job
To help me survive

Part 3
Where are you now the money's gone
Where can I find a home
Last night you were all around me
Now you don't want to know

How will I survive so far from home?
Can I get a job? I feel all alone
Last night was rich food, now it's
                                         scraps
Why don't I go home?

He wouldn't want to know me, I'm
                             sure of that
I've let him down so badly, and
                             that's a fact
No longer a son, but maybe a slave
What else is there?

The Road Back Home
There's a feeling inside me
That's calling me home
It says, 'Why should you stay here
In a land that's not your own?'
But though I see the sense of it
Somehow I feel afraid
I've made such a mess of my life
How can I face my dad?

And the road back home
Is a lovely one to travel on
When you know that you should
have stayed after all
But there's a voice inside me
That is leading me on
I'm going home, I heard the call

I don't know what'll happen?
What will he say to me?
How can I look in his eyes
And say, 'forgive me'?
I've done so much that's wrong
What can I hope from him?
I'll just say 'I'm sorry
Please forgive my sin'

Part 4
Now there is peace
Within his heart
Love has grown
While they were apart

The sights and sounds
Of his distant stay
Are no longer calling
For him to go away

His Father's eyes rejoice
To see him come
For life begins anew
Now he is home
* * *

AUGUST
Travelling South
on a train
Will it be the same again?

Something new
for me to do
Can it really be true?

August brings changes
new friends
on the beach
always in reach.

Going West
need a rest
Could this be best?

On the Coast
beans on toast
I love this the most

August brings changes
sometimes pain
sometimes rain
but always love
* * *

RUN FOR COVER
A million people terrified
Despair on every face
Hopeful dreams of tomorrow
Disappear without a trace
A distant sound of thunder
Sirens start to wail
And all the colours drained away
Everything is pale

In the night He is waiting
The eternal lover
When the sky begins to fall
You'd better run for cover

Why should we be the ones
To face the precipice
Could this be the final blow
We all hoped to miss.
Left without a turning point
Abandoned to our fate
Running out of possibilities
Waking much too late

Like pawns on a chessboard
Puppets tied with string
Dancing to our master's tune
The old familiar ring
But there is a different way to live
And there is one who cares
Everything is in His hands
And when we call He hears
* * *

TWISTED WORDS
Truth cannot be defined
Error doesn't matter
Lies aren't really sin
Listen to the patter

Twisted words, false ideas
Nothing's black and white
But corruption flees quickly
When exposed to the light

If you take my meaning
Values can be rejected
Hard and fast rules get in the way
They're to be suspected

The words you say are beautiful
The ideas are new
But don't expect anyone to listen
They won't believe it's true

We play our word games all the time
Breaking all the rules
But one day we'll realise
That we've all been fooled
* * *

HOLY FIRE
Holy fire, my desire
Come, I yield my life to you
Holy fire, my desire
Is to do the things I see you do

For you died to set me free
By your spirit make me what I
        should be
Holy fire, my desire
Fill me with your love so true
* * *

DREAMER

Your love goes on forever
No matter what I do
Each day it comes with freshness
Just like the morning dew

You don't see my shortcomings
There is no condemnation
And when the world is pressing in
You're there in my frustration

They call me a dreamer
They say it won't come true
But when the doubts surround me
I see the truth in you

The obstacles just melt away
Confronted by your power
And the dreams turn into reality
With every passing hour
* * *

DIFFERENT TOWN TONIGHT

Early morning at the station
Another tiring day
One or two farewells
And I am on my way

And Jesus you have called me
To reflect your light
Let your holy spirit fill me
In a different town tonight

I've been to this place once or twice
And the people that are so kind
But the seconds are so pressured
And I'm always short of time

One day the journey will be over
And there will be time to rest
But as long as you are by my side
I will give you of my best

NEVER MIND,
PRAISE THE LORD

How I wish the twinges would end
This pain is driving me round the
        bend
Never mind, praise the Lord!

One second it's a sneeze
Every other is to wheeze
Never mind, praise the Lord!

I always hope to do much more
They always seem to lock the door
Never mind, praise the Lord!

Wanted to go out today
But my friends have gone away
Never mind, praise the Lord!

And in my heart I know it's true
There is no problem too great for you
And though frustrations may appear
I know I need not suffer fear
For your purpose can never fail
And I'm on the victory trail

So if things are going wrong
Join me in this little song
Never mind, praise the Lord!

For I know there will come a day
When all our troubles melt away
Arid we will shout, 'Praise the Lord!'
* * *

SORRY

Sorry,
I didn't mean to say that
I didn't think

Sorry,
I don't love you anymore
I've changed my mind

Sorry,
I didn't want to steal
But they won't miss it

Sorry,
There's no money at the moment
One day we'll help you

Sorry,
I didn't mean to damage you
I just got carried away

Sorry,
We didn't give permission
For the bomb to go off

* * *

EXCUSES

I would have come
But the car broke down.
I am interested
But there's no time.
Yes I'm sure it's interesting
But I have commitments.
I'm sure it will be a good meeting
But I believe I'll be away.
I know I need Jesus
But any excuse will do!

PROMISES

We, the party, promise
that our promises are trustworthy
We promise to fulfil them
We promise that our promises
are full of promise
All other promises ever made
have never realised their promise
We promise that if elected
we promise to fulfil our promises, further more,
we promise that once in power
we will forget every promise we ever promised

MANIFESTO

We believe in free speech
You can say what you want
As long as you don't criticise us

We believe history has always been bad
There have always been the oppressed
If there weren't we wouldn't have a cause

We believe that everyone should be equal
That every man should have a right to his share
Especially those at the top

We believe religion should be abolished
What you don't know can't hurt you
And anyway, God gets in our way

We believe the world needs changing
If we fail by any chance
We have the weapons to make sure
No-one remembers

TRADING PLACES

If you were me
And I were you
There'd be so much
That we could do
Climb a mountain
Sing a song
Fight good battles
Walk all day long
But that's not how
It's meant to be
Rejoice because
In God we see
He made you - you
And made me - me

* * *

CRISIS

In the darkness fears rise
Tired eyes
Wishing peace will come
A word
Crisis torn
Feeling worn
Hoping
Daylight comes
New hope
I can cope
With him

* * *

ALL THAT I AM

All that I am
My hopes and fears
My achievements and failures
My laughs and tears
Can be summed up
In the words I sing
Jesus
My Lord and King

* * *

THROUGH A VEIL OF TEARS

1. The Dancer
The music plays loudly
The lights are flashing bright
Crowds of people dancing
Another disco night

The D.J. cues the record
Chart topper next in line
Everybody on the floor
Hope you're feeling fine

And the dancer sits by himself
Hardly ever seen
People all around you
Discreet distances in between

He dreams of conversation
That someone will say 'Hello'.
When the party's over
Alone in his wheelchair, home he
will go

2. Young Lives
Oh she is so beautiful
She will have such fun
Skiing in the winter
Bathing in the sun
Beach parties, discos
Barbecues and trips
Surely she's got it made
Smiling face, kissing lips?

But deep inside there's something
wrong
A fear not yet full grown
Inside the doctor's waiting room
In a crowd she sits alone
Suddenly time is short
So much yet to do
Her head reels in confusion
Can this really be true?

Young lives full of hope
Where has it gone?
Joy has turned to sorrow
And when will it be done?

3. It could have turned out differently
On the park bench he sits
A bottle by his side
Lost in an alcoholic dream
In a haze he tries to hide
And it could have turned out
differently
If things had gone all right
He could have been a millionaire
Instead of being where he is tonight

She washes the dishes slowly
Looking back at her life
Two broken marriages
An endless pain and strife
And it could have turned out
    differently
It could have been a happy life
She could have had everything she
    wanted
Been a contented wife

The dole queue is getting longer
And the money is running low
And all the endless promises
Like a thousand voices shout
And it could have turned out
    differently
With plenty to go round
Instead of the endless searching
And the too familiar sound

In the church pew eyes half closed
She listens to the song
The words bring distant echoes
She hopes it won't last long
And it could have turned out
    differently
She wished life was good again
But how can you trust in Jesus
When all you know is pain?

4. Why?

I saw TV today
Millions starving to death
A girl who needs a kidney machine
A man taking his last breath

I read in the paper
There could be nuclear war
While taxes rise even higher
And there's no food for the poor

And, Jesus, all I want to know
As I sit and cry
If there is a God of love
Then tell me, why?

They say love is the way
Yet all I see is hate
And those who can't take care of
    themselves
Are left to their own fate

And yet I hear the same old words
They tell me God is love
If this is true them maybe it's time
He stepped in from above

5. The Garden

And in the evening
As the night drew on
Into the garden
They came one by one

Stay here and pray
You won't be lost
In the winning day

And on his knees
His hands lifted high
His tears did flow
As he began to cry

'Father your will is hard
But there's no other way
To serve you, Lord'

And as the day drew on they took
    him away
Mocked, beaten, scoured, his body
    had to pay
They nailed him to a cross, laid him
    in a tomb
But he appeared again alive in the
    upper room

And in the garden
The stone was rolled away
And as the sun rose
Dawned a brand new day

And on his body is the pain
And in his love
Life begins again

6. *See it through*
And there are days
When I cannot face anyone,
When every step I take
Meets a closed door

Sometimes the pain
Gets too much to bear
But then I turn
And see there's someone there

And you have given me your love
When it gets rough
And I'm weak
I find your strength enough

Let tomorrow come
I don't need to hide
In tears and joy
You are by my side

And the day will come
When the pain will cease
And songs of joy
Will echo in the peace
* * *

NEW YEAR'S DAY
A new day begins
Full of hope
Our expectancy high
Trusting we can cope
Full of potential
Trusting him
Who knows the way
We take a gallant step
On New Year's Day
* * *

CASH CRISIS
There's a bill before the House
Which could make all the difference
But it will never pass
Because of lack of money

There's a child who waits in hope
That a miracle will happen
But his life is running out
Because he's no resources

There's a big crowd at Greenham
But the planes are flying in
Weapons its hoped we'll never use
A war no-one can win

Wed like to help those in need
But it's a case of rising prices
So I'm afraid you'll have to wait
Till the end of the cash crisis
* * *

AND FINALLY
Cruise missiles installed
Heightening of fear
International crisis
Armageddon's near
Fighting in Grenada
War in Lebanon
Peace talks falter
Protests carry on
Nuclear danger
In everybody's thoughts
And finally
Here is the sport
* * *

THE DAY AFTER
The sun broke through the clouds
Swirling winds of dust
Ash carried along in the air
Silence
No voice
Still
No movement
Quiet
The war over
Buttons pressed
Finished
But no celebration of laughter
For this is the day after
* * *

WHEN THE WIND BLOWS
Shadows fall across the sun
Civilisation quakes
The earth begins to tremor
Another tragedy breaks

Life for life that's the deal
Love is treated like a joke
Pollution gathers in the clouds
Watch the people choke

The blueprint is missing
The outcome no-one knows
But everyone will run for shelter
When the wind blows

Hatred, violence, pain and loss
Raise their ugly head
The fugitives of life
Fleeing from the dead

Strange sights at midnight
Lightning in the east
See the magic number
Issue from the Beast

Sirens in the afternoon
Alarms begin to ring
There's nowhere left to run
How will you face the king?

Distant clouds are shattered
The end of all our fear
Sounds of songs rejoicing
The coming one is near

PARADISE POSTPONED
Everywhere there are things you want
People have all the things you don't
Satisfaction is hard to find
And there is never peace of mind

The cut and thrust of life really hurts
Why is it always you who hits the dirt?
Can there be a way to escape?
Or is it just an everlasting tape?

But there is one who shows us how to live
That it isn't what we take but what we give
He made a path, He shows the way
Yet we ignore what He has to say

But can we turn our backs
On all we've owned
Or would it be a case of
Paradise postponed?

* * *

TEARS OF THE WORLD

Verse 1:
The rain is pouring
The sky is grey
Will there be more heartbreak
Another sorrowful day?

Verse 2:
There are people who walk the streets
'Cause they haven't got a home
And there are those amidst the crowd
Who are so alone

Chorus:
And there's one who hears them crying
As the rain begins to fall
And He calls for us to end
The tears of the world

Verse 3: There are days full of hunger
For the crops have failed again
Yet we cannot find a use
For the mountains of grain

Verse 4: There are missiles in the ocean
And satellites on the moon
But where will we stand
With Judgment Day coming soon?

Verse 5: For He taught us to love
And He showed us how to care
And He gave us His life
Which we should share
* * *

DANGEROUS LOVE

Everybody's looking, looking for love
But they're full of fear
Don't give yourself away
Don't let anyone hear

Just take what you can
Don't worry about the rest
Ideas are for dreamers
Be happy with second-best

But there's one who gave us everything
When He came down from above
And if you want to find reality
You've got to take His dangerous love

His spirit will fill your life
And you will be free
To live the life he called you to
And be what you should be

There's no room for resistance
Surrender to Him
And His love will flow through you
And give you peace within

The world is waiting to be loved
Can't you hear His call?
To break the power of misery
He demands our all
* * *

NO ONE WILL TAKE THE LOVE AWAY

Of all the love
I've ever had before
I give you everything
You gave me so much more
All the doubts have gone
Of you I'm sure
That your love is the best

You pick me up
From the cold hard ground
Dazed and confused
You brought me round
Turned away the nightmare
With love's sweet sound
And in you I rest

Chorus: Whatever the problems I meet from day to day
No one will take your love away

Hold me close to you
Through the longest night
I fear no enemy
You have won the fight
From the darkness of loneliness
You gave me sight
Jesus, I need your love

* * *

A LOVE BEYOND COMPARE

They look at me with pity
They say it's such a shame
All his life in a wheelchair
Isn't anyone to blame?

They wonder how existence
Can be so endured
Or seek for an escape route
Wishing I were cured

Please open up your heart
There's so much I can share
I've found a meaning to my life
In a love beyond compare

They only see the negative
Oh! how will he cope?
But my life is full of changes
Which speak volumes of hope

There is a power greater
Than any of life's pains
And even nailed to a wooden tree
He broke all bondaged chains

Nothing is impossible
When love is on your side
He has opened every door
And I am free to ride

Chapter 6
Between The Lines (1987)

Alyn says: Sometimes you feel good, other times you don't. A virus can really knock you down yet you trust in God to give you the strength to fulfil his call, even in the wind, rain and mud of Greenbelt.

We live in a world of tensions where there are more questions than answers. Where innocent by-standers are involved in the conflict, there is no escape. We are trapped between the lines and our only hope is the One who came to set us free.

These poems talk about the issues we face from day to day. Alyn continues to make progress. In the last year he has moved into his own accommodation and travels extensively.

He is sure of the fact that Jesus Christ makes a difference to life. From a position of hopelessness He has brought Alyn to a place of fulfilment in spite of frustration, and He stands by ready to rescue us from the worst of situations.

Alyn is available to come to speak or read poetry and distance is no problem.

LISTEN

You can hear it in the wind
As it blows through the trees,
There are words of wisdom
Carried on the breeze.

You can see it all around you
In the people that you meet
On the faces of the people
That we meet along the street.

You can see it in the dancing
You can hear it in the song
And if our ears are open
The words are clear and strong.

Listen, very carefully,
You can hear it in every way.
Listen, pay attention
God is speaking today.

APRIL FOOL

Thinks he's worked it out
His mind is clear
There is no doubt.

He doesn't realise
He has a hungry heart.
He couldn't see the truth.
He's never made a start.

He says he can't see God,
And thinks he is so cool.
But there'll come a time
When he'll see he's an April fool.

He builds his world on logic,
Trusting only in what he can see,
But the chains of oppression are invisible
Only Jesus can set you free.

There was a man on a hill.
People thought he died in vain.
But they didn't know the punch line
'Til he rose from the grave again.

LITTLE CHILD LOST

If I could talk to you
I'd tell you things you've never heard
About the greatest love
Who is God's living word.

If you would open up
He would take away your fear
He would answer all your questions
And show you He is near.

And all you want is love
But you can't face the cost
While you ignore the signals
You'll be like a little child lost.

There is no easy way
For you to find your dreams
But he knows your anguish
And hears your silent scream

He's waiting to surround you
With His constant peace
If you'll only turn to Him
Your wandering will cease.

* * *

GREATEST LOVE

I will sing to the ocean
Shout to the stars above
Something's happening to my life
I've found the greatest love.

Always been a dreamer
But I could never see
That other people's happiness
Could happen to me.

Always been the exception
The one left behind
And though I searched intensely
Priceless treasure I could not find.

But then one day in desperation
I saw him standing there
He took away my anxiety
And now I rest in his care.

If you're looking for happiness
Open your ears and hear
The love you're looking for
Is very near.

MORNING STAR

When I think of your love
I am so amazed
It exceeds all my hopes
And it leaves me dazed.

When I think of your love
And I begin to see
How you gave your life
So that I would be free.

When I think of your love
And the peace that you give
You have renewed my heart
And called me to live.

But I cannot express
How great you are
But I love you Lord
You are my morning star.

* * *

EVER DANCE

Can't you hear the music?
Don't sit still.
Let his Spirit touch you
Let him fill.
Every part of you
Will be set free
See the signs of change
Be what you should be.

Ever dance
Can't you hear his beat
Sing his song.
Get on your feet
Music is so sweet.
Feel his love descend
Come on and join the dance
That will never end
Ever dance.

My life was in ruins
'Til he came along.
But he changed the record
And gave me a new song
Can't you see his hand
Reaching out to you?
An open invitation
To dance eternity through.

CHILDREN OF THE WORLD

See the children playing in the sun
Happy smiling faces having fun
There are those who cannot play
the game
Yet they are children just the same!

Not children of a lesser god
Let them take their place.
They rely on you and I
To bring a smile to their face
Children of the world.
Children of the world.

Spare a thought for those who
cannot play
Facing pain and sorrow every day.
All they need is patient love and care
Surely that's not much for us to share.

Not children of a lesser god
Let them take their place.
They rely on you and I
To bring a smile to their face
Children of the world.
Children of the world.

Jesus has welcomed everyone
Every daughter and each son
Don't forget that we are children too
We all need love to see us through.

Not children of a lesser god
Let them take their place.
They rely on you and I
To bring a smile to their face
Children of the world.
Children of the world.

* * *

HANDS OF THE CLOCK

Waiting for something to happen
Sitting with bated breath
Watching the seconds tick by
As slowly as death.
Frustration like a tap dancer
Makes a heavy sound
Hopes struggle to reach the sky
Like heavy weights pressed to the
ground.

But the hands of the clock are restless
Though sometimes it's hard to see
But our trust is never in vain
And our longed-for dreams will be.

* * *

AFTER THE FIRE

1. Troublemaker
Nobody wants to hear your words
Why don't you go away?
Why do you have to disturb us?
We don't need to hear what you say.

Nobody wants a prophet
With a message of doom
Surely there are other countries
Who will give you more room?

We don't need troublemakers
Or warnings from the Lord
Just let us live our lives
You make us really bored.

2. The Waiting game
The ground is parched
No sign of water there
The food is running out
The heat too much to bear.

The signs of desperation
Show on every face
Authorities looking for hope
Going from place to place.

Don't let the rain fall down
Upon this barren land
Until the people turn
And begin to understand.

The weeks turn into months
And everyday's the same
And will there ever be an end
To this waiting game?

3. The Showdown
The people gather round
Ready for the fray.
A spectacle for free,
An epic match of the day.

They dance and sing and cut themselves
Shouting to their god.
But he doesn't seem to be listening
It seems so very odd!

Perhaps he's gone on holiday
Or maybe just asleep!
Or just far too busy
To answer those in his keep.

Now the time has come
And everything is ready
The altar is repaired
And his nerve is steady.

A quiet prayer ascends
To his Lord on high
And instantly a flash!
Fire from the sky!

4. Panic
They're looking for me.
Where can I hide?
Who will protect me,
Who is on God's side?

I've got to get away
Or else I will be killed
It's so hard to understand
Is this what you willed?

I will flee to the desert
Or to the mountain of the Lord
Perhaps I'll find the answers
Listening to His words.

I see a mighty wind
And an earthquake shakes the ground.
A flaming fire before me,
But He's nowhere to be found.

But then a gentle whisper
Echoes in my ear.
A voice asking a question
"What are you doing here?"

5. Go back
I'm pouring out my heart
To One who understands.
Who knows my every danger
And holds me safe in His hands.

The opposition's mighty
I need not be afraid.
No one can stop His purpose
Destroy the plans that He has laid.

"Go back", He says "and tell them
That my love for them is true.
If they will turn to me
I will bring them through.

They will never be defeated
For I am the Lord of all.
And they will share my victory
Go back and raise the trumpet call."
* * *

KNOWING
Knowing me, knowing you.
I find your love is true
Even in the depths of despair
When I call, I know you're there.

Even before my life began
You had already formed your plan
There is nowhere I can go
Whether high or whether low.

Knowing how much
You love me
There's nowhere else
I'd rather be.
* * *

ENCOUNTER
Wandering lonely as a cloud
Looking for a point
Drifting endlessly in space
Like an addict with a joint.
Suddenly I see a Man;
Imprint in His feet and hands
Then I know He's calling me
I hear His commands
He touches deep inside
My heart is free again
His life He spent for me
To end all my pain.

* * *

FEELING GOOD
In the morning
I wake to hear your voice
Your love touches my heart
I feel the pleasure of your presence
The sunshine brings warmth
And I feel good.
* * *

PROMISED LAND
We talk of justice
Fare shares for all
Equality's our goal
No one should fall.

Why are the hungry dying in the
streets?
Why has the beggar no shoes on his
feet?
If all are special I don't understand
Why doesn't it feel like the
Promised Land?
* * *

REFLECTION
By the water's edge
I see a reflection
A face I used to know
Full of youth
Eyes bright
No tracks of tears
Full of hope
Dreams waiting to be fulfilled
I turn away
Wishing to be young again
Free and innocent
Then I hear a voice
And realise
I am.
* * *

VICTORY SONG
Mary went to the tomb
To say her last goodbye
To the one she loved so much
And had watched him die.

But the stone had rolled away
In the early morning light
And the tears began to flow
'Til the Master gave her sight.

Sing a song of victory
All of us can now be free
In the upper room he drives away
                    the gloom
Now we see that Jesus is alive.

As they walked on down the road
They talked of what they knew
And then a stranger joined them
And showed them what was true.

And at the evening meal
In the breaking of the bread
Their hearts began to glow
For he was no longer dead.

Sing a song of victory
All of us can now be free
In the upper room he drives away
                    the gloom
Now we see that Jesus is alive

Since that glorious day
The world has felt his love
For we share his victory
And his Spirit as a dove.

So sing the victory song
For it will never cease
Let his power touch our lives
As we receive his peace.
* * *

CRY
See the broken people
Can't you hear their pain?
Who will lift their spirits
Help them rise again?

Millions spent on weapons
A war no one can win.
Millions die of hunger
Can't you see it's sin?

Cry for justice, cry for peace
It's time for war to cease
The man on the cross
Gave his life for us
Cry for justice, cry for peace

Greed and desperation
Investment and capital gain
But no one hears the cries for help
No one feels the pain.

But one day he will return
To see what we have done
Will we hide in shame?
Or will we stand before the throne?
* * *

STAND UP AND FIGHT
Can't you hear the sound of war?
It's knocking at your door
And you cannot get away
There's no place to hide
Now it's time to decide
Can't you see here comes the day?

Don't fear the darkness
We belong to the light
The battle is raging
Stand up and fight!

So much pain and misery
People dying to be free.
Can't you see tears of despair?
Who will come to their salvation?
What will be their destination?
Does anybody care?

Soon the battle will be done
And the victory will be won,
Of that there is no doubt.
We are soldiers in his power
This is our triumph hour
Very soon there'll be the victory shout.
* * *

HEART OF THE CITY
In the heart of the city
The shadows are falling down
Walking through empty streets
Silence is the only sound.

The clock strikes midnight
Night is on the run
Just a few more hours
And we'll be in the sun.

And our hearts are crying out
Will we ever get away?
But the shadows are already fading
As night gives way to day.

Searching for meaning
What is life meant to be?
In our dark confusion
How will we ever see?

There's a voice on the wind
And he turns the night away
Reaching out through the city streets
He shows the way.

There's love in the heart of the city.
                    * * *

TOMORROW

1. The Vision
It could have been a vision
Or was it a dream?
It seems so strange
What can it mean?

I saw him standing there
With eyes of fire
And as his spirit took control
I was lifted higher.

He said, 'speak of what you see,
Tell my people what is to be'.

2. Hold On
Tell my people
The hour is not long
Keep in the light
Don't do wrong
Don't turn to evil
Or listen to lies
Fear not your enemies
None of mine shall die.

Hold on
And I will give you victory
Stay close
Hold fast to my liberty
Though the times may get hard
And in darkness it's hard to see
Hold on to me.

3. Give us peace
When will there be an end to trouble?
When will the sorrows cease?
Death on every corner
Destruction's off it's leash.

Strange sights at midnight
And everywhere is fear
What happened to the sunshine?
Could it be the end is near?

Rumours of battles
Earthquakes in the news
Attempts at reassurance
Clash with opposing views.

The world is out of control
Who can tell when it will ease
In the night you hear the cries
Give us peace.

4. Don't Listen to him
Don't listen to him
He'll tell you lies
He'll promise sunshine
In the dark grey skies

All he wants is your worship
If you'll wear his sign
If you trust in him
It will all be fine.

Don't be taken in
By his conjuring tricks
Just wear his badge
It says six, six, six.

He offers you peace
An end to war
But if you give him your heart
You won't live any more.

5. *War*

Did you see the armies going to war?
I've never seen so many soldiers
       before:
Every people, tribe and nation
Gathered for the fight.
But in the midst of the battle a
       blinding light
A rider on a white horse
Crowns upon His head
One word from His mouth
And His enemies are dead
The battle is over
Hear His people sing
He will reign for ever
He is the King of Kings.

6. *Nowhere to run*

The time has run out
There's nowhere to go
You stand before His throne
Knowing what you know.

The Book will soon be opened
Will your name be inside?
Can you look into His face?
There's nowhere you can hide.

Time and time He's called you
He's shown His love to you
No matter what you thought
Now you know it's true

There's nowhere to run
You are on your own
Will you live with Him forever
Or face eternity alone?

The Amen

And I saw the city
Beauty beyond compare
Its streams of living water
Healing all the nations there.

I saw all the people
Stand before the throne
He wiped the tears from their eyes
And called them His own.

He said to me
'I'm coming soon
To put an end to sorrow
Tell my people to wait for Me
It will soon be tomorrow'.

* * *

ALL I NEED

When the rain is falling down inside
and I cannot bear the pain
When my life is coming to an end
You rescue me once again.

And even though I don't deserve it
By your love I am freed
When the world is falling down around me
You're all I need.

You picked me up when I was broken
My blinded eyes just couldn't see
Chains of desperation 'round my heart
And only you have the key.

No matter what may come my way
I will put my trust in you
And I will rest in your strong arms
Surrounded by your love so true.

I THOUGHT THERE WAS A SANTA CLAUS

I thought there was a Santa Claus
Who rode upon a sleigh
Who fulfilled all our wishes
On a snowy Christmas Day.

They talked of red-nosed reindeer
And of a secret place for toys
Of letters travelling through the air
From little girls and boys.

But when I opened up my sack
There wasn't what I'd hoped for
While everybody else was running around
For me it was a bore.

It's nice to think we get
Our wishes fulfilled
But what about Afghanistan
And thousands being killed.

Yes, I thought there was a Santa Claus
Who rode a magic sleigh
But I've never got out of my wheel chair
On a snowy Christmas Day.

* * *

GO

They say I'm a failure
A hopeless waste
Object of pity
Rejected
They wonder how I can cope
Feel sorry for me
Pat me on the head
Offer to buy me an ice cream
But they never talk to me.
Did you have a good holiday?
Do your really travel alone?
Aren't you brave?!
So clever.

But there's One who commands me to go
And tell of His love
No matter what obstacles
And I will go in His power.

* * *

FIRST CLASS

Looking through the window
At the pleasant countryside
Rushing through the heather
Seeing Scotland's pride.

A week-end in Aberdeen
Going to see some friends
People all around me
Coping with sharp bends.

Sounds of joy and laughter
Appreciation of good food
Tourists over from the States
Don't want to be rude.

The hospitality's great
But I feel like little Jack Horner
Nobody seems to have time
For the table in the corner.

* * *

HAPPY EASTER

The sun is shining
There's a warmth in the air
Spring is coming
Summertime is near.

Chocolate eggs in the shops
It's time for lots of fun
No more work till Tuesday
I'd like a hot cross bun.

But what about the empty tomb
And don't forget the upper room
The hands of Jesus, blood and scars
Breaking down death, iron bars.

Happy Easter to everyone
Life begins with God's Son.

* * *

PRESENCE

I feel so good
Because You're there
When I'm frightened
You take my fear.

You've done so much for me
More than I can say
And Your love is getting stronger
And better every day.

I've just got to let You know
How much I love You
From the edge of darkness
You've brought me through.

So never let me go
I would never survive
It's only in Your presence
That I am alive.

* * *

WORDS

If I had the words I could express it
But I haven't
It's a mystery
Even a sentence
A phrase
A comma
A letter from the alphabet
But there's nothing I can say
Just
I love You.

* * *

ALWAYS THERE

When I look at my life
And I see what I have done
And I wonder if the problems
Will ever be over and done.

And when I hear Your voice
Then the conflicts inside cease
For You turn away the angry storm
And bring Your gentle peace.

So let the night fall down
I won't have any fear
When I call Your name
You're always here.

I don't know what will happen
What the days ahead might bring
It may be tears or laughter
I may cry or sing.

When the pressures get too much
You'll hold me in Your hands
And Your love will surround me
And in Your strength I'll stand.

When it gets too much to bear
There's a place that I can hide
And there's One I know who'll care
Who will never leave my side.

* * *

THANK YOU FOR THE MUSIC
Fleetwood Mac in the background
Singing a familiar song
Words I've heard before
Please don't get me wrong.

Music is my passion
I want to tap my foot
Dancing in my spirit
Sitting in my seat.

Rhythm in my heart
No time for the blues
You gave me a new song
Changed my blue suede shoes.

I want to sing your praises
Say how great you are
I want to sing the Jesus song
Playing my guitar.

So thank you for the music
Let me always twist and shout
Jesus you love me
So let me sing it out.

* * *

IN YOUR EYES
What a hopeless case
Associate member of the human race
Little value anticipated
Kindly, patiently tolerated.

What future can there be
Achievement can't be a reality
No hope, they do not fit
It's a waste and that is it.

But You're the One who heals the
pain
It's You who brings to life again
You break the barriers on every side
And welcome those who are denied.

For You came to end the lies
And we are perfect in Your eyes.

BETWEEN THE LINES
1. The Book
From a word came a sentence
From a passage came a fact
In a list of directions
And a way to act
Into my hands it came
A book with no name
And a voice that said "Read"
Listen
A voice
Pointing to the past
Talking of the present
Signing the future
Words
Psalms
So I opened the book.

2. Back to Eden
In a world of desperation
Broken dreams and desolation
Can we find a way to live our lives?
What happened to the peace we had?
Why has all the good gone bad?
Now the ploughshares have turned
to knives.

See the storm clouds gather
We're a children without a father
Gates are closed, no way back home
All our hopes have turned to dust
What was gold, now is rust
And we are so alone.

And our hearts are crying
For we have lost the garden
And cannot find our way
Back to Eden

What will become of us?
Is there any point to fuss?
Or is destiny beyond control?
The death sentence has been passed
Judgment cannot be suppressed
Is there anyone who can make us
whole?

3. Midnight
Midnight
All is dark
Dogs bark
Babies cry
People die
All alone.

Midnight
Fears rise
Weary eyes
Shadows fall
Strangers call
Don't follow

Midnight
Wishing
Hoping
Some other way
Yet dreading day
It could be worse.

Midnight
Does someone care?
Is love there?

4. Loneliness of the worst kind
Tear down the fortress of pretence
It doesn't get us anywhere
How long can we sit on the fence?
Is there any reason why we should care?

How do we get out of here?
Who knows the way we should go?
Does anyone listen to our cries?
When honesty comes, it hurts so.

Is there anyone who can bring us
              peace of mind?
And end this loneliness of the worst
              kind.

We struggle on to find a way
Hoping for a golden age
But our dreams shatter like glass
And optimism too, turns to rage.

How long will we have to wait?
Will it be 'til the end of time?
Broken hearts in a sea of tears
Going on right down the line

5. Scenes from a movie.
Boy meets girl
Falls in love
Happy marriage
Falls apart.

Talented girl
Broken life
Cancer victim
Wonders why?

Hungry people
Water dry
Governments spending
Watch them die.

S.D.I.
Talks of peace
Another war
World turns on.

They're just scenes from a movie
Everyone can see
Just reflections of reality
What else could they be?
Just scenes from a movie
Or are they?

6. Bite the bullet
Don't let your weakness show
You must be strong
No room for emotions
Whether they're right or wrong.

We've got to bite the bullet
Got to be a tough guy
Take the road to recklessness
Whether we Iive or die.

We've got to turn a blind eYe
To sorrow and pain
Don't let them see you cry
They won't trust you again.

Be quick on the draw
Shoot first then see answers
Don't waste a second
We don't get many chances.

The whole world is hiding
This is our high noon
No room for turning
The reckoning is coming soon.

7. *Top priority*
There's a well without water
There's a field without a crop
Yet the lights are burning brightly
Dripping taps spill many a drop.

There are many without homes
Children dressed in rags
There are many sleeping under bridges
Houses made of plastic bags.

It's a simple operation
And with it they could live
But there are more important things
For which we're told to give.

There's a satellite in space
Which will keep us free
It eats millions of dollars
And is given top priority.

8. *Looking for a hero*
Call in the F.B.I.
We need assistance
We're being overcome
It's time for resistance.

Send a message to Superman
We're on the brink
Perhaps they'll come from outer space
So that we don't sink.

Looking for a hero
Will we live or die
But no one seems to answer
We can't work out why.

Is there any hope for us
The situation is grave
Will we be annihilated
Or will we be saved.

We're reaching out in desperation
Where have all the heroes gone
Just when we needed them
We can't find one.

9. *Prodigal world*
The world is turning
Out of control
Over a precipice
Falling down the hole
Murder, extortion
Robbery, rape
Nuclear destruction
With no escape.

It's a prodigal world
Violence on the loose
With the trap-door sprung
Head in the noose.

Tears of anguish
Howls of pain
Longing to be
Retrieved again
Media hype
The music's gone sour
Storm clouds gather
For the final hour.

But back in time
The fool on the hill
Turns the world upside down
For he is living still.

Prodigal world look and see
His death on a cross
Has set you free.

10. *Only love can change a heart*
When you are near me I feel real
Your love breaks through and I am
healed
The shadows shrink and I can see
And you're everything to me.

Take me from darkness to the light
I give you my blindness, give me sight
I feel your presence every day
I know that you will not ever go away.

Only love can change a heart
Only you can make me whole
All I need is you beside me
Fill my soul.

Your song is music to my ears
It takes away my doubts and fears
Keep me safely in your hands
And in your power I'll stand.

Fill me with love that I can share
Tell them there's someone who
               really cares
Now everything makes sense
Against the bad times your mind
               defends.

11. *Between the lines*

Well, I used to have an easy life
Which was free from care
Hoping it would all work out
The answers would be there.

I sought the sound of laughter
And didn't see the tears
Full of optimism
Ignoring my fears.

But now I see the battle
The rain on every side
The pleasant days of yesterday
Have run away to hide.

The armies are gathered
For a fight to the end
And when I look around me
I see no one else to send.

And I'd rather be anywhere
Than where I am right now
I'd no weapons to fight with
And I don't know how.

But how can I be indifferent
When I've seen the signs
So I'll stand until the victory's won
Here between the lines.

12. *Here comes tomorrow*

I heard a sound on the wind
Good news for every ear
The answer to all our questions
Will become very clear.

A new age is coming soon
Filled with joy and laughter
All our hopes will be fulfilled
A happy ending ever-after.

So wait for the morning
There will be an end to pain and sorrow
The clouds are breaking
Here comes tomorrow.

We don't have to wait too long
And we have a part to play
Learn to love and to care for each other
And it will speed along the day.

The story is nearing it's end
And now we know the right direction
We've been through the depths of
               death
And now it's time for the resurrection.

Alone on a stage
I see them look and stare
See their puzzled faces
An enigma in a wheel-chair.

You took my broken body
And made me live again
You give me power to live for you
Through frustration, fear and pain.

Sometimes I don't understand
The things you put me through
The odds are all against me
And yet you bring me through.

They only see the laughter
But you wipe away the tears
It's you who picks me up
When I'm drowning in my fears.

And though there may be problems
I know your love is true
And whatever I may face
I'll do anything for you.

* * *

Chapter 7
If It's Friday... (1989)

Alyn says: Sometimes it's hard to remember where you came from or where you are going. The good news is that I had a new home and new beginning, the bad news was awkward journeys by train wondering whether you could get there on time and be met by the people you trusted.

INTRODUCTION

It has been my privilege to have known Alyn over the last couple of years and particularly in our work together on university and college missions. Alyn has more determination and drive than anyone I have ever known and his vision for what god can do through him is very exciting. Anyone who has met Alyn will know what I am talking about.

Throughout our work together, Alyn has demonstrated his capabilities as a speaker, (and comedian), but one of his greatest talents is as a poet, not just in writing but in performance. His presentation of poems such as 'WHO AM I?', 'THE DAY DEATH DIED' and 'SO WHAT NOW?', all of which are in this present volume, at recent missions have left people deeply moved and stirred to look at this God of love, proclaimed through suffering and frustration. The privilege has been mine. May this book make you stop and think and come back again to the outstretched arms of the risen Jesus.   Rev. Dave Rowe

VOICES
Waiting for an answer
The question not so clear
Voices are shouting
But I just can't hear.
Give me your answer
Help me find the way.
Too busy with word games
But some of us cannot play;
Suddenly a new voice,
Now I understand
No longer confusion
For you are in command

LOVE LED ME ON
Love led me on
From my isolation
Broke through the walls
Of my frustration
Opened the door
And set me free
Caused me to blossom
And let me be me

Love led me on
To people and places
Gave me acceptance
In welcoming faces
Made me feel valued
With a part to play
Filled me with hope
Each dawn and day

SENSIBLE PEOPLE

Sensible people all around
Keeping their feet on the ground
Miracles; a thing of the past
A change of heart will not last
But two thousand years it goes on
Despite discoveries love has not gone
Sensible people can't you see
He is the beginning of reality

* * *

LOVE IS

Love is a word
A familiar expression
A fashionable ideal
A dangerous occupation.
Love is being forgiven
Resting in your arms
Knowing I can rely on you
Assured of your promises for ever

* * *

SITTING

Sitting on a door step,
Watching the world go by
No one seems to notice me,
But I wonder why.
Could it be I scare them
Because I am not the same?
Perhaps the word 'spastic'
Carries terror in it's name.
If they would only listen
I would proclaim Your loving care
Your power in hopelessness
And presence always there.
But until their minds are open
They will only see the lie;
So I will sit on the door step
And watch the world go by.

* * *

WHERE I BELONG

I feel your love everywhere I go
There is something I want you to know
I need you right here
To take away fear
I have found the place where I should be

My life is in Your hands
And my heart sings a new song;
In Your loving arms
Is where I belong

Peace of mind is what You offer me
You died to set the whole world free
You will not let me fall
And answer when I call
There is nothing more I could ask of you

* * *

IS ANYONE THERE

Can you hear the sound of fear
Marching down the street
Looking for an exit
Heavy running feet

Anguished voices crying
How did we go wrong?
Prophets of doom abound
The end may not be long

As the storm clouds gather
Hearts filled with fear
Call to the sky
Is anyone there

The truth has been revealed
Many times before
But you padlocked your heart
When he knocked on your door
Now it is so different
The stakes are very high
Time to face the question
Will you live or die

* * *

RETURN TICKET

I bought a ticket to paradise
But it caused me such pain ;
The ticket was a return
So I could not remain.
Just as I was settling down
Looking forward to my food
Someone said the taxi is here
The awakening was quite rude.
But I have another ticket
And this time I can stay
The Station Master paid for me
And it only goes one way

* * *

IF IT IS FRIDAY IT MUST BE LIVERPOOL

If it is Friday
It must be Liverpool
It is so hard
To be Your fool
But with Your power
I know I can

In this crowded carriage
Feeling all alone
I cannot understand
Why I am known
Just a mystery
That I am in Your plan

And I know when I get there
There is so much we can share
For broken hearts and lives
Will look to You

So if it is Friday
It must be Liverpool
For You give me strength
And keep me cool
I will bring your love
To everyone

BROKEN TOY

Broken toys
Shattered dreams
Endless rage
Silent screams
No hope found
Darkest night
Then a sound
And You the light

MAGNIFICAT 1

Paradise lost
For the sake of pride
Afraid to look
Instead we hide
Can the wrong
Be put right
Is there an hope
It's the night?

MAGNIFICAT 2
Follow me to the ends of the earth
Let me show you what you are worth
Let your heart be strong and true
So that your eyes see what I can do
Don't ask questions just obey
There will be blessings on the way

MAGNIFICAT 3
The time of night is over
The day springs forth with joy
Good news for God's people
The birth of a humble boy
A King will come to rule
To wipe away the tears
He will bring peace and justice
And drive away our fears

MAGNIFICAT 4
An end to war
Promise of peace
Hatred destroyed
Fighting to cease
Justice will flow
Like rivers of old
A time of plenty
Where each shall have gold
A Promise fulfilled
From ages past
A kingdom of righteousness
Built to last

MAGNIFICAT 5
A message from God
The time of salvation
A new beginning
Beyond expectation
In submissive obedience
She answers the call
Carries inside her
The Saviour of all

MAGNIFICAT 6
'No room at the inn'
The owner said
Only some straw
In a cattle shed
No royal palace
No proclamation
Just cattle sounds
For the Lord of creation

MAGNIFICAT 7
The sky was bright
A dazzling sight
As shepherds watched sheep by night
Words of comfort did they speak
A Saviour for the low and meek
And so in Bethlehem they did seek
The good news for all men

MAGNIFICAT 8
Herod's fears began to rise
With the news from the skies.
Foreigners came to see a king
Expensive gifts they did bring.
Yet while the enemy prepared His
plans
The baby was safely in God's hands

MAGNIFICAT 9
The light will shine for evermore
For He has opened heaven's door
The child grows up to be a man
Giving His life to complete God's plan
He sends His grace upon us all
But will we answer to His call?
From heaven He came to lift us high
To pay the price lest we die
Sing praise to God and magnify!
Emmanuel comes the Lord most high!

* * *

WHO AM I?

I ask the questions that no one wants to know
I look for directions
Wondering where to go
I hope for fulfilment
A reason for being
But all I get is nothing
Like eyes never seeing
Tell me who am I?
Why am I here?
Do I have any value?
Is there anybody there?

TOUCHED BY LOVE

Touched by love
And what was ugly
Turns to beauty

Touched by love
Tears subside
Replaced by streams of joy

For I find meaning in you
The world becomes a different place
Where I am at peace

Touched by love
No longer guilty
Your power gives me life

NORMAL PEOPLE

Your eyes say it is okay
Your smile bids stay a while
You feel safe
There is no danger
You give acceptance
Not seeing a stranger
But you have mis-read the story
And overlooked the twist
The trouble with normal people
Is they don't exist

DEEP

Deep as the ocean
Sings a silent song
High as the heavens
All the day long
Like roots of a tree
Your love is found
My heart is quickened
When I hear its gentle sound

THE BORDER

Wire and trench lie ahead
Running for life
Escape from the dead
Don't look back
No regrets
What will they say
Can I forget?

Flashlights pierce the darkness
Sirens wail
Must keep going
Or I will fail
Crossing the border
Surrounded by pain
On the other side
Life begins again

SO WHAT NOW

So, what now?
Do I walk away
Save your love
For a rainy day?
Programme time
In my filofax
Treat it all
As just old hat?
But what about the fact
Of your generous act
Dying in my place
To take away disgrace?
Surely I can't forget
Your love is calling yet!
So, what now?
I give my life to You!

* * *

ONE DAY

One day
I won't have to apologise
Cope with staring eyes
Be an object of pity
Have difficulty in the city.

One day
They will understand
The situation is in hand
That I really have a brain
Not an escapee from the insane.

One day
I will be treated as human
The way God sees me now

* * *

GENESIS 2

Entrance
The city waits
Expectant gates
People cheering
Authorities fearing
Songs singing
Bells ringing
He is here!

Betrayal
A last meal
A dirty deal
Unseeing eyes
Fooled by lies

A moment in time
A sour rhyme
Misplaced trust
Hopes turned to dust

A secret sign
At the end of the line
Betrayers hand
Fulfils what is planned

Angry voices
Angry voices crying
Faint hearts sighing
Innocence condemned to death
The world holds its breath
While breaking hearts
Wish for another way
Hoping for a brighter day
But the verdict
A forgone conclusion
Darkened sky
Amidst confusion

The day death died
Were you there
The day death died?
Did you feel
His wounded side?
Did the peace
Renew your hope
So that you could cope?
Did you hear
The broken chains
Feel the perfume
That heals all pains
Find our heart
Begin to fly
As life began anew
Nevermore to die?

* * *

WHAT'S THE POINT

What's the point of being good
Of always doing what I should?
Nobody keeps the score,
Don't understand what it's for.
Is there any reason for belief
Does it bring sweet relief?
Yet thousands find it true
When they need help to get through.
So what's the point of being here
If there isn't anybody there?

1989

The angels cry
The heavens sigh
False promises are made
As we live a lie.

With all hope gone
We struggle on,
But fear the finger
On the button.

And we like to feel
That we're doing fine
But the clouds gather
Nineteen-eighty-nine.

Can you hear the call
As the weak hit the wall
While power is misused
And little ones abused.

But there will come a time
We will see the sign
No one knows the hour
Maybe nineteen-eighty-nine
* * *

IF I ....

If I was a singer
I would sing beautiful songs.
If I were a dancer
My feet would tap the rhythm of life.
If I were honest
I would admit that I fail.
If I had common sense
I would come to you
And receive acceptance.

REALITY

What is reality?
Where can it be found?
We send rockets into space
We tunnel through the ground.
We ask awkward questions
Hoping for a clue;
Trial by jury
Weighing up what is true.
But where is reality
Will we ever see
A man with outstretched arms
Saying, 'come to me'?
* * *

EVERY MOMENT

Every moment is special
A gift from heaven above
A treasure beyond compare
Celebration of his love.
Tears of joy,
Shouts of laughter
Sad stories
Happy ever after
Each one priceless
A golden treasure
Grace unbounded
Love beyond measure
* * *

STREETS

Approaching midnight
The temperature drops
Shadowy figures shelter
In doorways of shops.

Chilly winds blow
Bodies for hire
While cozy at home
We sit by the fire.

Out on the highways
Where the crossroads meet
We need to take love
Into the streets.

There's no use pretending
The job is done
There are millions of hearts
Waiting to be won

ST PANCRAS BLUES
Waiting for a train
Heart full of pain
Oh, not again!
People crowd around
Hear the mournful sound
Strikes on the underground.
More delays!
And the tannoy keeps speaking
And it's all bad news
While I sit and wait
With St Pancras blues.
* * *

TRAFFIC LIGHTS
I wanted to make a start
To really go places
To meet lots of people
Friendly faces.
I was full of ambition
A real go getter
Always looking for an angle
To make things better
Put here in the traffic
I can't get ahead
The engine is revving
But the traffic lights are red!
* * *

EUROPE
I ordered egg and chips
And I got coq au vin
That's what happens when you join
The Common Market
* * *

THOUGHTS
I think therefore I am
But what am I?
Why am I here?
I think I am important,
Valuable,
But perhaps these thoughts are wrong
Can anybody tell me
What I should be thinking?
I think God cares
I hope I'm right

DISTANT CRIES
You watch the T V
And hear the news
Comforted by experts
Soothed by their views.

'It's not up to me'
Is what you say
Leave it to God
It'll be OK.

But can't you see
You've been fooled by lies,
And we can't wash our hands
Of the distant cries.

There's a need for action
That includes you and me.
If we open our eyes
We will see:

He showed us the way
By his dying breath
And his power will give us
Victory over death
* * *

REFUGE
When the world asks too much
And I cannot cope.
When I'm feeling alone
And losing hope.
When I wonder how long
Before the dream comes true.
When frustrations surround me,
I look to you!
And your love
Like a river
Overflows
Fills me with confidence
Helps my faith grow.
For I know you will keep me
In the midst of the deluge
Safe in your arms
For you are my refuge

* * *

Chapter 8
Never Ending Stories (1991)

Alyn says: It's good to have wheels and somebody beside you. It opens more doors and begins a new chapter. Me, my friend and my Astra travel all over the country.

Foreword

It is a privilege and a joy to commend my friend Alyn Haskey. Ever since we were students at Theological College in 1978 I felt that Alyn was a unique servant of the Lord. He is great fun to be with, full of patience and perseverance. Because Alyn is in a wheelchair he is labelled disabled. Dis-abled! Alyn is able to do a great number of things that many abled folk can't do. He has so much ability it comes out of his ears. (How many degrees has he got?!) He is a man of prayer, a preacher and a poet, more than that, the Lord's unction is on him.

J John, Nottingham

BEAUTY
Beauty is in the eye
Of the beholder:
A slim figure
Trim face
Nimble waistline;
We appreciate these.
When figures bulge:
Features fade
And nimble waists expand.
The heart given to God
Endures forever
* * *

LAMENT
Working for the Lord
The pay may not be good
But there are compensations
Like friendship and lots of food

Coffee morning over
Waiting eagerly for lunch
Anticipation high
Tasty morsels to munch

The fare is set before us
And joy is tinged with pain
I can't believe my eyes
Quiche and salad; yet again!
* * *

A BIG MAC SATURDAY
Munching a quarter pounder
Sitting in a corner
Waiting for coffee
That never seems to cool

Surrounded by high street people
Confronted by choice
Upstairs, downstairs.
A desperate milkshake
Decides to commit suicide
By jumping into a shopping bag.
Frantic parents
Encourage children to behave
With threats of death or worse.
The lady with the mop
Provides a regular service
Washing the floor
And customers feet!
Meanwhile, Donna wipes the tables
And wonders if there could be
More to life than this.
* * *

DANCER
The music stirs
Rhythms haunting
But a simple task
Seems so daunting
He longs to fly
To break the air
But tied to the spot
In his wheelchair
The dancer sits
And waits for the day
When with his love
He will waltz away
* * *

INSANITY

Twenty thousand soldiers
Marching as to war,
Banners flying high
Mighty cannons roar.

Twelve thousand soldiers
Won't come home again,
Pride has turned to shame
Joy has turned to pain.

Eight thousand soldiers
Marching home to stay,
The game is called insanity
And anyone can play

* * *

TERRACES

They came in thousands
To enjoy the game,
They left in despair
Lives never the same.
Like the crack of a whip
Bitter pain stings.
Yet though crushed and broken
Still the spirit sings,
And hope is still alive
Amidst the loss and pain
Like a phoenix from the ashes
Their song will rise again.

* * *

YOUR LOVE

Your love touches deep within
Restoring my hope.
I see the beauty
Transformed from darkness
Strength returns
And defeat recedes
Your love brings me to victory,
And You

* * *

THE SONG REMAINS THE SAME

The melody lingers
Chords reach a crescendo
Though not the joyful music
Of youthful days

Yet the theme is strong
And the song
About your love
Remains.
For on that day
You rescued me,
You gave Your life to me;
And so throughout the years
I sing without shame
The melody You gave.
The song remains the same.

* * *

TEARS OF A CLOWN

You see a smile
And joy fills your heart
The laughter lifts you
But look behind the mask
And you will see I'm down.
Look deep into my eyes
And see the tears of a clown.

* * *

EXILE

Where are the promises
I heard of in my youth?
So many lies abound
I long to know the truth.
Why has it all gone wrong
In this wilderness?
I feel so alone
Father take me home.

Restore again, oh Lord
The days when we did sing.
Let the sound of laughter
Through the city ring.
Lord, this exile is so long
Through this desert
I am forced to roam
Until you call me home.

Let your righteous anger
Turn to acts of love
Stretch out your hands to heal
Send peace as a dove:
Then I will sing a different song.
Show me your mercy,
I bow before your throne
For you have brought me home.

ONE SECOND
One second leads to the next
And I begin to see
How you poured your love
Out upon the world
Not seeking anything
In return
But to spend
One second of eternity
With you!

* * *

END OF SUMMER
End of summer
And leaves begin to crinkle.
The sun thinks about flying south
For a mid winter break.
Holiday romances are forgotten,
Despite promises to write.
Hopes and dreams are put away
In cases for next year
And only photographic memories
Keep alive our hope
That summer will come again.

* * *

ARE THEY REALLY
He is a student you know!
Is he really?
With little speech
And no control
How on earth can that be?

She is an athlete you know!
Is she really?
In her wheelchair
How can she compete?
Well, fancy that, I do not see.

They are married you know!
Are they really?
How do they cope?
It must be hard
Not like you and me.

They are human you know !
Are they really?

* * *

SHOPPING
Home again!
A cup of tea
Now the rush is all over.
Check the list
With satisfaction.
Feeling all in clover;
Cards and stuffing,
Pipes for puffing,
Fairy lights and tree,
Turkey, crackers, scarlet ribbons,
Drinks and guide to the TV.
Yes, it is all here!
Nothing left to remember.
But what are we going to do
For the rest of September!

* * *

WRITINGS
There are days
When I wonder
If anything
Will work out
I struggle over words
Feeling the emotions
The heartbreak
Frustrated anger
Lonely fear
Wishing
I could express myself
Put on paper
The hopes and dreams
In my heart
Using the gift
You gave me
Hoping to change the world
I sit at my computer
And wait for Your love
To release the energy
That will touch someone's heart

* * *

FLAME
In the early morning
I look for you
To wipe away my tears
And show me what is true.
Running on empty

You fill me once again,
You break the shackles
And put an end to pain.

And I can't live without you
It would not be the same
You keep me burning brightly
Everlasting flame.

I want to tell the world
Of everything I've found
You pull me from the pit
Set my feet on solid ground

* * *

YOU REIGN

You reign
The earth declares your praise
The heavens sing your glory
No one can count your days
Your love goes on forever
And you will never die
You are exalted
For you reign on high

* * *

LIGHT

Darkness covers the earth
Hearts broken by hate
Dreams crumbled to dust
Fear resigns to fate
Hope turns to nightmare
Words of empty release
Pain is ever present
Never seems to cease
But wait
A voice
Singing in the night
Good news
For everyone
Here is Light

* * *

FORWARD

A new year begins:
Looking back I rejoice
Your love did so much.
In the mirror
I see a difference,
Rough edges are smooth
Tears are wiped away
And the broken shell
Is slowly being restored.
But that was yesterday
And I cannot stand still.
Ahead is the unknown
Changes and challenges
An uncharted region
There is fear.
But with you
I go forward.

* * *

GILDED CAGE

I lack for nothing
My life is full
Excitement abounds
Life is never dull
I am envied by people
For all I possess
They think I am happy
They can never guess
But I see the bars
That hold me tight
In my gilded cage
Bathed in sunlight

* * *

A TOUCH OF LOVE

A touch of love is all I seek.
To be accepted, not seen as weak
A place of belonging where I am free.
Won't someone reach out rescue me?
A touch of love to save my life
When the pain of rejection cuts like
a knife.

* * *

HOSTAGE

There are no chains
No doors to hold me in
I am free to move
Yet I am a prisoner
To eyes that stare
Whispering tongues
Negative attitudes
Constant devaluation
And a body that fails
These are the things
That hold me down
Yes, I am a hostage
But my heart is free.

* * *

DESIRES

Sex, money, rock and roll
Drugs to fill the gap in my soul
A flash car to get me places
Fashionable clothes; airs and graces
A well paid job
Vacation in the sun
Days of maximised profit
Nights of fun
I've got it all
Can't you see
I bet you'd like
To be like me

Sex, money, rock and roll
But who can I find to satisfy my soul
When the pain is too much
And the tears flood
The anxieties raging
And I don't feel good

Sex, money, rock and roll
I need somebody to make me whole.

* * *

INNOCENT BLOOD

The cry of the innocent
Hangs in the air
Shrieks of terror
A rage of fear
Exploitation,

Abuse,
Mistrust,
Beauty defiled,
Love turned to lust.
So save our children
From this carnage
Lets have no more
Of this ruthless damage.
God keeps his record
Of bad and good
And he hears the wailing
Of innocent blood.

* * *

BUT FOR YOU

But for you,
I would have given up.
Run away in retreat,
Died of frustration,
Accepted defeat.
Turned to crime
Or selfish greed,
Exploited others
Become a priority need.
But I saw your scars
And your bloody wound,
And you changed my heart
My life, my moods.
But for you,
That's how I would be:
But because of you,
I am free!

* * *

DECADE

Ten years gone
We move on
Looking back
See the facts
War and peace
Never ceased
Falklands, Ethiopia,
Revolution in Eastern Europe,
China crushes democracy;
But the human spirit never dies.
In the face of famine
Hearts reach out with love.

Aids is a killer
Yet death also stalks
The hungry, rejected and poor.
Sometimes hot
Mostly cold
But is the earth becoming a
                    greenhouse?
We say 'Farewell' to those who left us
Yes, ten years
A decade
Good and bad
What will the next one be like?
                    * * *

RISING
In the distance
Warm rays of light
Chase away the shadows,
Pushing back the night.
Rumours abound:
An empty tomb is seen.
Fact or fantasy?
What can it mean?
Hearts are rekindled
Fear is cast away.
Peace, hope and power
For us day by day.
                    * * *

POINTING FINGERS
Pointing fingers
Words of reproach
Whispers behind backs
Accusations flying
Pictures of judgment
She didn't did see
How could he
Always blaming
Pointing fingers
While He who could condemn
Says 'Go in peace'.
                    * * *

THE RIVER
I'm going down to the river
To get my fears cast away

Been surrounded by sorrow
Every night and day
Haven't had any joy
Nightmares all the way

I'm going down to the river
To get myself made clean
Always been so selfish
I've got a heart that's mean
And I feel so unworthy
Guess you know what that means

I'm going down to the river
To see a man who can make me real
With a touch of His hand
He's got the power to heal
And He's waiting for me
Knows exactly how I feel
                    * * *

LESSONS
If only I would listen to You
Then maybe my life would be different
I would not make so many mistakes
Have to apologise so often
Not get embarrassed
When the things that I do wrong
Come to light
I would not feel guilty
Or have to hide
There would not be any condemnation
But I've never been very good at
                    listening
And it's only your patience
That keeps me
In Your presence.
                    * * *

RAP
Walking along
Singing a song
Feeling good
Like I know I should
Touched by your love
Heavens above
You set me free

So that I could see
How much you care
That you're always there
Blessing my life
You take away the strife
I have your peace
And I feel at ease
I know you died
But you're glorified
You conquered death
With your dying breath
And you rose again
And broke my chain
And you're always around
Like the sweetest sound
That's why I'm walking along
Singing this song.

* * *

I CALL TO YOU

I reach out to you
And I hear your voice
Giving me direction
In the midst of choice
You calm my fears
And take away the doubt
Fill me with your love
And call me out

Won't you hear my cry
Show me what is true
Chase away the nightmare
I call to you

You are my guide
Help me find a way
When the clouds are stormy
On the darkest day
I want to live for you
Glorify your name
Whatever the situation
You are always the same

* * *

SIGNPOST

Where am I going?
How long will it take to get there?
I need to know your truth
Guide me;
Show me Your ways.
I long to please you
Your love has touched my heart
And you are my hope.
All day I will follow
If you will show the way.

* * *

NEVER ENDING STORIES
LIFE

From the darkness
Power reaches out
A word is spoken
A command, not a shout,
Light springs forth
Night and day
Stars in heaven
Their beauty display
The pulse quickens
Warmed by the sun.
A smile of satisfaction.

FOLLOW

I will give you all you need
I will bless you all your days
You will find the riches of life
If you follow my ways

The plans I have are perfect
They will bring you joy and peace
They will take away your fears
And make your troubles cease

SO FOLLOW ME

I will shower you with love
Give you hope for tomorrow
Follow me

Let me hold you in my hands
And show you many things
Fill your heart with laughter
For I am the King of kings

STORM CLOUDS

From east and west there gather
Fire in the sky
Hopes and dreams tormented
How could we live a lie
All he said is happening
Fear on every side
A nation sent to exile
Because of guilt and pride

REJOICE

There is a whisper on the wind
That hope is born again
And the eyes of the blind
Can see again

The lame are walking
Broken hearts are healed
Gods love has come again
His promises are sealed

Rejoice, rejoice,
The man from Galilee
Has broken all our chains
So we can be free!

As He rode into the city
Songs of joy were heard
Not only from the people
But from the stones and birds

But there was opposition
And a traitor told his tale
And the One who came to save us
Was handed over in a sale

BLOOD, SWEAT AND TEARS

Blood, sweat and tears
Mixed with fears.
A sense of betrayal
And one who had failed,
Crowds of people
On a green hill
Even though he is dying
They mock him still.
Clouds of darkness,
Trembling hearts,
Yet there is peace
As he departs

EARLY MORNING

Sadness and sorrow
They walk to the tomb
Shadows stalk with fear
All is gloom.

But the body is gone
Not a trace is found;
Just a shaking earth
And a distant sound.

As the sun comes higher
Day is dawning
And he rose again
In the early morning.

Though at first, in fear,
They ran away
Their hope was certain
By the end of the day.

DAYS

She wonders what life is for;
Has it always been this way?
The heavy drudge and monotony
Never having a say.

He hopes for something different,
Perhaps a brighter life,
An end to all the problems
Which seem to be so rife.

They find it boring,
Always the same,
Is this the only reason
Why they came?

But there's One who offers hope
And an escape from the maze
If we will reach out
He will fill our days

DRIVING

The music plays softly
As motorway lights soothe;
Miles tick by
And soon we will be home.
I feel the comfort of your warmth
And know how much you love me,
I am content,
Enjoying your words
And your presence.
There may be many miles yet
Before my arriving,
But as long as you are here
I am happy to go driving

Chapter 9
The Promise (1992)

Alyn says: Things don' always work out the way they should. When you rely on somebody the worse things are mishaps but God is good and He compensates and gives new things.

FOREWORD

Being vulnerable is something lots of us talk about and recognise as a 'good thing', but because it's costly, we sometimes choose to walk another way. Alyn has the gift of standing like a mirror before us, reflecting back to us things we are afraid of in ourselves, exposing things we would prefer to keep hidden.

His poems are uncluttered and unadorned, accessible to everyone; indeed, it is their simplicity that takes you straight to the heart of the matter. Thank you Alyn - and I haven't forgotten that, just like David, sooner or later we'll be dancing together before the Lord.

Pippa West, Liverpool

APRIL

Icy tentacles hold tight
Yet the sun will have none of it
Birds are singing
And everywhere life begins anew
Winter is receding
For April has come

* * *

LOVE

As the day goes by
Let love grow stronger
Hearts joined together
Lasting longer
Sharing with each other
Joys and tears
Finding comfort
Against the fears
Love at the centre
Joy and peace
Blessings from heaven
That never cease

* * *

LOVE IN A DYING WORLD

Take a look around you
Tell me what you see?
Fear on every face;
How can that be?
Clouds of dark pollution,
Choking up the sky.
'Who has the solution?'
Many voices cry.

And it's no good to look away,
You know there's a better way
We need love in a dying world
Today.

There is so much starvation;
What on earth can we do?
Leave it to the authorities
Forget about me and you.
But every time we show love
A miracle occurs,
And our complacent indifference
Only makes it worse.

Let love be genuine
No more selfish pride
We need to look to others
And take their side.
There's a man way back in time
Who showed us the way
Gave His life, for love.
We need to give our love away

SPRING

The sunshine warms our hearts
Love is kindled
Hope springs forth
Dreams of good times to come
Fill our minds.
The seaside
A city full of tourists
Remind us that summer is near
And the darkness of winter
Packs its suitcase
And takes a long vacation
Until autumn

* * *

AT ANY MOMENT

At any moment
Love may come into your life
It may be a smile
A word
A common interest
Sharing a drink.
When it happens
Receive it with joy
Take pleasure in its presence
For it is not ours to keep
You may wish the day not to end
But it must
And who knows about tomorrow
But there is this hope
Love once visited
May come again
This time to stay

* * *

MORNING WORLD

The sun creeps from behind the cloud
Smiling with warmth
Rays of light touch the earth
And birds sing.
Flowers open their eyes
And reveal their beauty,
Another day dawns.

* * *

QUESTIONS

Will today be like yesterday
Full of pain
Disappointment
Heartache
Failure?
Or will it be different
With hope
A promise
Success
Encouragement?
Only you know.

* * *

SEA BREEZES

I do like to be beside the seaside
Watching the waves crash to shore.
I do like to feel your love around me
And know I am secure.

* * *

FIRST IMPRESSIONS

Eyes look with approval
Or disgust
They take in the style
Of clothes and hair
They look for signs of breeding
They turn away
Not wishing to be caught up in the pain
Or count the cost of commitment
Eyes look
But they don't see the real me

* * *

LONGING

I have a longing
To be free
To be accepted
Seen as me
No longer guilty
But at peace
To see the battles
Within me cease
I have a longing
To be approved
Safe from danger
And always loved

REVELATION

You think I am your worst nightmare
A total catastrophe
When you look at me you feel ill
And wonder how such a thing
Could happen?
If God is love
The cost is too high
And yet guilt forces you
To try contact
Then you discover
I am like you.
* * *

WINTER

Dark nights surround us
Icy fingers squeeze
Our hearts shiver.
We draw our coats tighter
As the chill bites;
But soon it will be Christmas
When life begins again.
* * *

EXCEPT FOR ACCESS

I could have danced on a stage,
Sung songs of hope,
Been an encouragement to friends,
Performed a service for mankind,
Scored a winning goal,
Been a responsible citizen,
Carried the hopes of the nation,
Healed the wounded,
I could have done great things!
Except for access.
* * *

PEACE

Pour Your peace
On troubled water.
Let the wounded soul
Find rest.
No more striving
No more conflict
Heal the heart
That has been stressed.
Like a river,
Overflowing,
Wash away the strains of life,
Turn our mourning into dancing
For you are victor over strife
* * *

TEN YEARS AFTER

Life changes;
But still they stare,
Talk in loud voices,
Giggle behind hands,
Converse with my keeper.
I am still expected
To do nothing,
To be happy and grateful.
A symbol
Encouraging others.
Life changes
But ten years after
It is still the same.
* * *

NO COMPROMISE

No compromise
We stare across the table
Blaming each other
Eyes like daggers
Not seeking forgiveness or
Reconciliation
As military force gathers
With weapons of destruction
Pushing diplomacy
To the background.

No compromise
As nails are driven into hands
Tongues speak words of hate
And He dies
for all!
* * *

REACHOUT

I heard you calling
Telling me of your love
Making me feel valued
I have never heard
These words before
So how can I refuse
When you reach out to me

* * *

SCATTERED THOUGHTS

There are so many questions
                in my head:
Are you alive or are you dead?
Who is really in control?
What will happen to my soul?
Can you really give me peace?
When will all fighting cease?
If I call will You answer me
And open my eyes so I can see?

* * *

HERE COMES THE SPRING

Every day the darkness
Relinquishes its hold
Shadows slink away
Confronted by sunlight
And lighting up time
Gets later.
Soon it will be safe
To walk home again
Without having to rush
For fear of night.
Teatime will be in daylight
And we will say
'He comes the spring'.

* * *

HANDS

Take my hand
And put it in yours
Hold me close
Let me feel your love
Place your hands
On my brow
Taking away my sin
Close your hands
Around my life
and never let me go

IT SHOULD HAVE BEEN DIFFERENT

It should have been different really,
I think it's all gone wrong.
The solution should have been easy
But it's taking far too long.
I had the right intention
Determined to see it through.
But something must be missing
I haven't got a clue
Yes
It should have been different really,
And it's making me feel blue;
For I want to finish the job
But I don't know what to do!

* * *

THE PROMISE

Disaster
A time of pain
A period of grief
Enemy action
Disbelief.
A distant cry
Where is hope?
At the end of the tether
Who can cope?
Where is God?
What will he do?
What of the promise?
Will he see it through?
Look at the heart
Don't look for strength
Or a pleasing face
Boundless energy
Or even grace.
For my ways are higher,
I told you that from the start,
Forget the outward things
Look at the heart.

Here is my Servant
He will do My will.
I know you have questions
And you doubt me still
But I know what I'm doing
So why not be smart
Don't look at his age
Look at the heart

Only a Shepherd Boy
Only a shepherd boy.
What is he doing here?
Surrounded by confusion
Doubts and fear?
He wants to make a stand
But it seems absurd,
Plenty of courage
Lets take him at his word.

Only a shepherd boy,
The armour won't fit,
It seems impossible
That he could make a hit;
But a twirl of his sling
A stone aimed at the head
And the object of our fear
Falls down dead!

Jealousy
Jealousy rears its ugly head
Desiring vengeance
Seeking to destroy
Causing friends to part
Spilling blood in every direction
And even when spared
Showing no gratitude
Jealousy kills

Tears
Tears flow down from the sky
Wise men sit and wonder why
Warfare rages on every side
And those who lead us have all died.

Let tears flow like a river
With never-ending pain
As we cry out 'Who will save us
And give us life again?'

The bitterness of destruction
Is so hard to bear
Yet hope comes from the ashes
To drive away our fear.

It is the time of destiny
And all eyes turn to Him
The promise now fulfilled
The Man born to be King.

Celebrate
Fling wide the gates
Jerusalem will sing
The nation is united
And here comes her king.

The glory of the Lord
Shall shine upon this place
The blessings of the covenant
And His saving grace.

So celebrate, celebrate,
Let us dance and sing
For our God gives us the victory
And our Lord is King.

Temptation
While the army is away
Kings are tempted to play.
Attracted by beauty and warm desire
Not heeding the danger of the fire.
Trapped in sin,
The deadly curse,
It leads to deception
And even worse
And only the voice of righteousness
Makes him repent and confess.

Wash me
Wash me, Lord,
And make me clean.
For I know
That you have seen
What I have done;
Has caused you pain.
Cleanse my heart
And start again.

Wash me, Lord,
And hear my song
I have sinned
For far too long.
If you forgive me
I'll praise your name
And serve you Lord,
I'll spread Your fame.

Heartache
Heartache on every side
Sons revolt, children fight.
Those he loves turn away
Could it be he's lost the day.
Friends and enemies, all around,
Plot to see Him crash to the ground
And tragedy stalks in silent shoes
And will there be yet, good news?

My son, my son
My son, my son,
What have you done?
You were the fairest of them all
And now I've lost you
There's nothing I can do.
My son, my son,
Where have you gone?

My son, my son,
You've broken my heart.
What shall I do without you?
Did you not understand?
I held you in my hand
My son, my son,
Where have you gone?

Rest
Now is peace
A time for rest
Until that day
When all are blessed.
Sleep with our fathers
With guarantee
That your descendants
You will see.
Reign again
In glory and power
At the promised appointed hour.
* * *

O LORD
O Lord, I praise You!
Let the angels sing
Let heaven and earth declare
The wonders of my King.
For You are mighty
And You keep Your word
And throughout all generations
You are the Lord.
* * *

TV DINNER
Lets buy a TV dinner
Then we can watch the war,
Marvel at the technology
At sights never seen before.
And as we eat our food
And watch it round the clock
The taste will give us comfort
And wash away the shock.

IT SEEMS TO ME
It seems to me
That every time
I try to do something right,
That mishaps always happen,
And I end up in a fight.

It seems to me
The world would be
A much nicer place,
If we welcomed every person
As part of the human race.

It seems to me
That we could be
Happy and at peace.
If love was in our hearts
Then jealousy would cease.
* * *

CITY NIGHTS
The cold wind blows around
The streets are full of sound
Bright lights touch the sky
Whilst on pavement pillows lie
Those without a home
Feeling all alone
Some who cannot cope
Lost all sense of hope
These are the sights
You see on city nights
* * *

DREAMS
I wanted to be
An engine driver
Breaking the speed record
Keeping to the timetable
But now I sit and wait
For a train which is late
Again
* * *

SMILE
I like it when you smile
I forget for a while
The troubles in my life
The pain and the strife
Your eyes light up the sky
And I wonder why?

You are able to rejoice
When you have no choice.
Please tell me your secret
I promise I won't forget.
What love is in your heart
And how did it start?
Yes, I like it when you smile
For you do it all the while
* * *

FREEDOM
Freedom
Is not being able to do
What you want to;
Going for a walk,
Making small talk,
Having lots of things,
Cars, houses and rings,
A holiday in the sun,
A life full of fun.
Freedom
Is in the heart.
You need Jesus for it to start.
* * *

WARMTH OF YOUR LOVE
It's been a cold and lonely winter
I thought that I would die
I was drowning in my sorrow
Until You heard me cry.

You saw my heart was frozen
Emotions just like ice,
But the sun has begun to shine
And I'm coming back to life.

Living in the warmth of Your love
You wipe my tears away
And the shadows of the cold, cold night
Have turned to a summers day.

Now I see the signs of spring
And I walk in Your light
For the coldness of the winter
Has already lost the fight.

So pour Your love upon me
And always keep me warm
When icy fingers reach out for me
You will keep me safe from harm.

AS SURE
As sure as the sun rises
And the moon sets,
As sure as the mountains
Haven' t fallen yet,
Your love goes on
Without end
No matter what
Is around the bend.
For You have promised
And given Your word
So sure is Your covenant
For you are Lord.
* * *

UNTIL THE FAT LADY SINGS
I can see in your eyes
That you think I'm mad,
I've lost any semblance
Of sense that I had.

You won't believe a word
There is no chance at all
That my dreams can come true,
Surely they must fall.

And do you think I'll be counted out
When the bell rings,
But don't you know it's not over
Until the fat lady sings.

I won't give up my hopes
Or accept defeat,
For the enemies around me
Will soon be in retreat.

The power that I have
Doesn't come from me,
It is from the one who broke the chains
And set the whole world free!

Chapter 10
Ten (1993)

Alyn says: A new car, a new friend and new opportunities. It's good to see God at work.

FOREWORD

I have worked with Alyn on a number of occasions. I have always felt it to be a joy and a privilege. To say that Alyn Haskey is a poet is only part of the truth. In fact, he is a poem, a work of God's art, definitely a 'one off'.

Anyone who has heard Alyn read his own poetry will be ready for the simplicity and power of this collection. They will also have the advantage of memory of his self-deprecating humour, head on one side, wheelchair motionless in the spotlight, his tongue fighting to form the words.

Those who have not heard him in action will have to read the poems for themselves. The best of them are excellent. The rest are always powerful, authentic. There are places of pain and difficulty in every life. In his continuing pain and struggle, Alyn speaks for all of us. His poems become our voice.

Buy them; read them; ponder them. You will be enriched, stimulated and strengthened.

Eric Delve, Bristol

ROAD RUNNER
Speeding along
You don't hear a sound.
Moving so fast
Your feet don't touch the ground.
Running away
From what you can't face,
Trying to keep ahead
Yet trailing in the race;
Road runner stop
And look into his eyes;
He is the one
Who holds the real prize.

* * *

FIRE
Touch my mouth
That I may speak
To broken hearts
Estranged and weak
The guilty ones

Who have no hope
Those holding on
To a fraying rope
Lift their eyes
From the mire
To see your love
A blazing fire

* * *

WHEN CHILDREN CRY
When children cry
The sun hides,
Rain pours down,
Harmony turns to cacophony
And laughter runs away.
For this is not how it should be:
There should be joy,
The sound of singing
A deep trust
And love;
So don't let children cry

* * *

JUST LIKE THE SUN

Just like the sun
Your love warms my heart.
You dry my tears
And give me a new start.
You are my Lord and Saviour
I will praise Your name,
Let Your love shine on me
And make each day the same.

* * *

DANCE, DANCE

I'm gonna dance all day
For the Lord.
Tap my feet
Twist and shout
Sing His praise aloud.
I feel just like a river
Never sitting still
I'm gonna dance all day long
I want to do His will.

* * *

FREEDOM CALL

Freedom
This is our song
The chains are broken
That held us for so long
By His mighty power
Our enemies are gone.
Freedom!
Freedom from now on.

* * *

MISSED AGAIN

Your eyes sparkled across the room
I was captivated by your smile
We moved closer
But wheels
And footrests made it awkward
Cupid fired his arrows
But he missed, again!

* * *

YOUR LOVE

In the depths of despair
My eyes look to you
Crying for hope
Watching you pick up my heart
Restoring my dreams
Knowing that without you
Life would be a sick joke
Without a punchline
It only makes sense
When I have your love

* * *

MIDNIGHT

Shadows hover
Shrieks of pain
Demons rattle
Heavy chains
An icy finger
Down the spine
Your reflection
Or is it mine
Midnight comes
To bring us fear
But it fails
For you are near

* * *

LOST DREAMS

What happened to the girl
Who grew into a princess
What happened to the genius
Destined for success
Where did happiness run to
And the sense of peace
Life full of riches
Nights of rest and ease
Lost dreams keep surfacing
Flush them down the drain
But love can revive them
And we can dream again

* * *

SILENT RAGE
How could this happen?
Who can we blame?
No matter what we try to do
The result is the same.
Whatever happened to love
Peace and goodwill?
Isn't life supposed to be precious,
Why do we kill?
Would the story be different
If we turned the page?
Is anyone listening
To our silent rage?

* * *

WHY ME?
Overtime at work
Wish that I could shirk
It's always the same
Always get the blame
Why me?

No time to spare
But they know I care
They never lend a hand
I don't understand
Why me?

Nailed to a cross
Suffering such great loss
When I look into his face
I see he is taking my place
Why me?

* * *

DAYS OF LOVE
Let days of love
Flow like water
From a never ending source
Each one filled
With moments of treasure
As life takes its course
Let the flame burn bright
Even in the darkest night
Through happiness and pain
Till day breaks again

DON'T TALK TO ME ABOUT LIFE
Don't talk to me about life
I think it's just a joke
And I don't like the punch line
It makes me want to choke
Please stop talking
I don't want to hear
The truth might make me think
And that is what I fear
Don't talk to me about life
I really can't face it today
I'd have to make a decision
And live a different way

* * *

AM I AN ACCIDENT
They tell me I'm an accident
That is why I'm here
A succession of chances
Which is very rare
A mixture of gasses
Molecules and parts
A hit and miss affair
With many stops and starts
But if I am an accident
Can someone tell me why
I have such concern
About if I live or die

* * *

DREAMING
I'm dreaming of happiness
A life full of ease
Purpose and contentment
Laughter and peace
A comfortable existence
With treasure every day
But how can I find it
Who knows the way

* * *

THE LIGHT AT THE END
OF THE TUNNEL
The light at the end of the tunnel
Keeps shining bright
My eyes are fixed upon it
In the darkest night
Sometimes I think it's fading

And it may die
Then I start to worry
My heart begins to cry
But when I look again
I see it is still on
And I will walk towards it
Until my fears are gone
* * *

SECURE
When the waves crash against the shore
When my hopes collapse
And I feel unsure
Your love surrounds me
Bringing new hope
Your strength within me
Then I can cope
For Your promises stand
And Your word endures
And Your peace like a fortress
Means that I am secure
* * *

LOVE TAKES MY HAND
Love takes my hand
And I can stand
My foot upon the rock
What ever the knock
You forgive my ways
And fill my days
With sweet success
Tears and happiness
Your love takes my hand
Then I understand
How much you love me
* * *

SATURDAY LITTLE CHEF
Please can I have the Frank
I don't want to call it a Bill
Because when I see the prices
I know that I'll be ill.
After all that time in the queue
It was nice to get the weight off our feet
And it only took half an hour
Before we started to eat!
They said it wouldn't be long

And so I held my breath;
But I nearly died of heart failure
Saturday at Little Chef
* * *

YOUR ARE MY LIGHT
You touched my life
And chains fell apart
Fears ran away
You revived my heart
Took what was broken
And made it new
Gave me fulfilment
I trust in You
When I feel hopeless
And full of pain
You calm my fears
Reassure me again
That You will never leave me
In the midst of the fight
In my darkest hour
You are my light
* * *

SURPRISE
There was a man named Zak
Who wasn't very tall
So he climbed up high
To see above them all.
He thought that he was safe
Amidst the brown and green,
Then he heard a voice
And knew that he'd been seen.

When he heard the words
He was quite surprised.
Until that very moment
He'd always been despised.
From that special day
He was no longer sad;
He found out that God loved him
For no one is too bad.

Oh Zacchaeus,
Come down from that tree
I'm coming to your house
And I want some tea.

127

MIRROR IMAGE

In my weakness
I came to your window
But you turned away
Not wanting to know
You perceived my pain
And felt my despair
Acknowledged my existence
But wished me not there.
You wrapped me in love
And hid me away
And thought to yourself
They have nothing to say
But as you start listening
And seek what is true
You look at my image
And find that it's you

* * *

LIFE

Life is what you make of it
That's what they say.
Keep it to yourself
Don't give it away
Keep it in a box
With a lock so tight
Hide in the darkness
Shrink from the light
But freely he gave
And showed us the way
Life is for living
So start from today.

* * *

HOW CAN THEY REFUSE

If they could see
Your love for me
Your presence every day
Which gives me hope
So I can cope
Whatever comes my way.

If they could feel
Your loss and pain
And touch Your heart of grief
They wouldn't hide
From Him who died
Or live in unbelief.

And when they know
The hurt you bear
Hatred and abuse
The prize you won
Through your own son
How can they refuse?

* * *

QUESTIONS

Why does it rain
When I want to go out?
Why should I whisper
When I want to shout?
Why don't the answers
Come straight away?
Why do I struggle
Each and every day?
Is there someone who can answer
The questions in my head;
Or will the solutions
Remain unsaid?

* * *

PROMISES

You didn't promise me
Sunshine every day
An important job
Good wages
A comfortable house
A happy marriage
The best car on the market
Holidays on the continent
A sure fire pension.
You did promise
To be with me always.

* * *

WAITING IN THE WINGS

I am waiting in the wings
For my time to arrive
I am feeling dead inside
But You made me alive.
Disappointment and frustration
Are hard to bear
But I know I will cope
If You are there.

So I am waiting in the wings
For that special day
When You will clear the obstacles
Out of my way.

* * *

LIVING IN THE GAP
I've heard your word
And done my best
I've toiled hard
And now I rest
Changes will come
Ups and downs
But You will keep my feet
On solid ground
So I'm living in the gap
Far from home
Holding onto Your promise
Until I see it come

* * *

AUTUMN WINDS
Autumn winds blow
Cold enough for snow
Lengthening night
Chase away the light
Wintry showers fall
Hear November call
But soon it will be Christmas
And spring will come again

* * *

WITH YOU
I can face the terrors
Of the darkest night;
With my back against the wall
I will win the fight.
Surround me with your love
And there's nothing I won't do.
For You won the victory
I am alive with You

* * *

WINTER
The temperature has fallen
Clouds fill the sky
The sun rarely shows it's face
Pretending to be shy.
Shops are full of Christmas
Faces warm and bright
Decorated trees abound
Shining in the night
And in the deep midwinter
Amidst the snow and frost
We see those who are penniless
Homeless and lost.
And Jesus, gentle baby,
Promised Saviour, King,
Breaks the hold of winter
Promising the spring

* * *

DIRTY HANDS
Dirty hands, dirty hearts,
This is where the trouble starts
Filled with bitterness and spite
Not caring if it's wrong or right
Greedy desires to make things bigger
Itchy fingers on the trigger
Life is cheap, it doesn't matter
Place the bomb and watch them scatter
But wise is he who understands
His blood has cleansed our dirty hands

* * *

FOLLOW YOUR HEART
Dreams like confetti
Fall to the ground
The water rages
We are all but drowned
Pain is constant
Troubles increase
And only His love
Can bring us peace
When your hopes
Are torn apart
Feel His presence
Follow your heart

HALF LIGHT

The sun casts it's shadows
On scurrying people
For it is nearly time for tea
Reds and yellows
Highlight traffic jams
Shops begin to tidy up
And night stretches and yawns
For it is half light
And soon it will be dark

* * *

I THINK OF YOU

When the winter is so cold
When I'm feeling very old
I think of you.
When the sun is shining bright
When I dance in golden light
I think of you.
You touch my heart and set me free
Break the chains that hinder me.
And I know Your love goes on
I thank You!
When the tears are falling fast
I know my sadness will not last
I think of You!

* * *

WAITING

I am waiting for the sun to shine
The clouds to disappear
The trees to turn to blossom
The start of the new year
I am waiting for the pain to cease
For hope to rise again
When Jesus is the victor
Breaking my heavy chain

* * *

A NEW ME

I want a new me
Not like the old
Warm soft and sensitive
Not heartless and cold
A face always smiling
A heart all aglow.
Where can I find a new me
Does anybody know?

JUST A SIP OF COFFEE

I'll just have a sip of coffee
Then I will do my work
I promise to get it finished
Honest I will not shirk.
I like to sit and chat
And pass the time of day
But somehow it gets away from me
And time slips away.
Yes, I'll just have a sip of coffee
And I will be on my way
If I've got time this evening
I will try to pray.

* * *

MILES

Travelling miles
Friendly smiles
Interesting places
Welcoming faces
Speaking for You
In all I do
Receiving Your smile
In every mile

* * *

TELL ME YOU LOVE ME

Tell me You love me
That's all I need to know
That You will be with me
Everywhere I go.
Tell me You have a place for me
Where I will be at peace
Where You will wipe away my tears
And make my sorrows cease.
Tell me You love me
Each and every day
Then when the troubles multiply
I can make them go away.

* * *

SILENCE

Silence surrounds me
A peace beyond understanding
Where clouds dance upon the sky
Flying birds declare Your glory
The golden sun shows Your splendour
And You talk
In never ending words

* * *

TEN

One, for the joy that fills my heart
Two, for the wisdom that you impart
Three, for Your Spirit with me every day
Four, Your family I meet on my way
Five, Your faithfulness no matter what I do
Six, abounding patience when I haven't got a clue
Seven, a day of rest when I can hear Your voice
Eight, You give me freedom; leaving me the choice
Nine, Your life inside me through the victory of Your son
Ten, Your love around me like a raging river flows on and on

Chapter 11
Snapshots of Tears and Laughter (1994)

Alyn says: From coast to coast we travelled bringing the good news, a message of hope and love to the north, south, east and west.

FOREWORD

Alyn Haskey is one of my heroes. His creativity, determination and zest for life is infectious and inspiring.

His poetic creations arouse a diversity of emotions and spark a multitude of moods from reflection to laughter.

He is honest, anointed and gifted. I'm sure you will enjoy his book too as the one that you will pick up often to enjoy a refreshing oasis in the midst of a busy day.

I have worked with Alyn on a number of occasions and am proud to call him a colleague.

Lowell Sheppard
National Director, Youth for Christ

LESSONS IN LOVE

Teach me to be patient
And never lose control;
To disregard the obstacles
And press on to the goal,
Not to get angry
When things don't work.
Give me perseverance,
When I want to shirk.
Teach me of Your love
And all you have to give ,
Show me your ways
So that I may live.
* * *

WHOSE EARTH IS IT ANYWAY

Whose earth is it anyway?
Who gave you the choice?
You think you own the planet
Don't listen to the Master's voice.
Cut down all the trees,
Put poison in the air
And as long as there's a profit
You haven't got a care.
But it should be a place of beauty
Of healing and of rest

You take what you want to
Making sure you get the best.
But one day you will realise
That it isn't just for you
God gave His gift to everyone
And we all live here too.
Whose earth is it anyway?
It belongs to the One
Who gave His life for all of us
Jesus, God's own Son
* * *

CONSTANT LOVE

When the sun shines
And I feel good
I know I'm acting
As I should
When darkness comes
And I'm afraid
Forces disrupt
The plans I laid
I turn my eyes
And look above
And reach towards
Your constant love
* * *

JOURNEY'S END

Let me see Your power
In my life each day
When the storm clouds gather
Make them go away

I feel Your love inside me
And know Your Word is true
Fill me with Your Holy Spirit
I want to be like You

Jesus, I love You
Will You be my friend?
Always walk beside me
Until my journey's end
* * *

FREEDOM EXPRESS

He heals the sick
And raises the dead
Feeds the hungry
With fish and bread
He calms the storm
And walks on the sea
Now he says 'follow me!'

Our sins are forgiven
He drives away all fears
Makes us feel welcome
Brings joy from tears
He died in our place
And lives today
So we can be free

Come on board
    the freedom express
You don't need a ticket to ride
We're on our way to the promised land
With Jesus as our guide!
* * *

BOOGIE DOWN

I want to boogie down
To the King of Kings
He fills my heart
With songs to sing
He gave His life
So we could share
The wonders of love and care.

I feel His rhythm
Hear the beat
I cant stop dancing
Need to move my feet
His Spirit is with me
As I go on my way
And I will boogie down
            night and day
* * *

THE EXTRA MILE

Will it be tomorrow
When I will finally know
The wonders of Your grace
And which way I should go?
Will it be this year
When You will take my hand
Break the chains that bind me
And allow me to stand?
I have so many dreams from You
And each one takes a little while
But as long as You are with me
I will go the extra mile.
* * *

IN THE BEGINNING

In the beginning
You spoke and there was light
Oceans and land
Day and night
You looked with contentment
On all You had done
Then handed it over
To everyone.

In the beginning
There was damage and sorrow
Days full of tragedy
No hope for tomorrow
A life without meaning
Body out of control
Then You spoke
Now I am whole.

* * *

COFFEE, CAKE AND COMFORT

Coffee, cake and comfort
With a sugary silver spoon.
We talk across the table
Hoping our trials will be gone soon

You talk of your frustration
Looking back across the years,
Of all the pain and heartache
The sorrow and many tears.

I talk about what might have been
Of dreams that have gone wrong
High ideals gone missing
Promises broken for so long.

The words of consolation
Seem to dull the pain a while
To bring a twinkle to your eye
That causes me to smile.

So it's coffee, cake and comfort
When next week we meet again
Yet we never do invite the One
Who came to heal our pain.

SUMMER GONE

Summer gone
The wind whistles round my feet
The sun has lost it's heat
The days are growing cold
The earth is feeling old
The leaves begin to fall
And I hear winter call
But your presence every day
Feels like summer's here to stay.

* * *

LOVE LIGHT

All alone in the darkness
Surrounded by fear
Reaching out for Your hand
I know that You are near
Your love just keeps me going
Whatever comes my way
For You turn the darkest night
Into the brightest day
And as long as You are with me
I will never lose the fight
When the shadows fall around me
You are my love light.

TAKE ME ON

Take me on
To higher ground
Let me hear Your gentle sound
New horizons come in sight
Guided by Your loving light
Turn my back on what is past
Forgetting that which does not last.
Take me on
On wings so free
and show me what
You plan for me.

* * *

THAT'S WHAT HE CAME HERE FOR

There's a glow in the air
And a smile on every face
A season of good wishes
For the human race
There are lights in the windows
Ribbons on the trees
And no-one seems to mind
If the weather should freeze
Christmas songs are sung
And we think of days of yore
But when January comes around
Will it be just like before
A baby born in a stable
There's a knock upon the door
Love comes to stay forever
That's what He came here for.

* * *

TIME

Tick tock
My little clock
Seconds pass
Through the hour glass
Helter skelter
Run for shelter
A distant shout
Time has run out

* * *

LOST YEARS
Who will turn the clock back
And wipe away the tears
Mend the broken hearts
And banish deep held fears
Overcome injustice
Hatred and abuse
Bring a sense of value
Instead of 'you are no use'.
To Him they were not forgotten
For He always hears
Now is the time for healing
For all those lost years.
* * *

DOES IT REALLY MATTER?
Does it really matter
What I say or do
If the things that I believe in
Are false or true?
Is anybody listening
Or taking note of me
Will it change their lives
Can it set them free?
Does it really matter
Do we have a choice
Or should we be living
At the guidance of His voice?
* * *

ONE OF THE CROWD
I'm very proud
To be one of the crowd
It's nice to be accepted
My opinions are theirs
And we always share
No-one likes being rejected
We follow like sheep
Talk is cheap
For safety comes in numbers
I don't want to stand out
Because it carries no clout
And, well, you just feel lumbered
So I am very proud
To be one of the crowd
And follow the leader each day
And I'll push back the fears
That ring in my ears
That say - is this the only way?

I'VE GOT NEWS FOR YOU
I've got news for you
Something's going wrong
Someone changed the manuscript
Now we're singing a different song
Jobs are on the slide
Money's gone down the spout
Some are living on the streets
Others are dining out
Hope has gone on holiday
The future's looking dim
We're running out of time
I'm not sure if there's life Jim
I've got news for you
There is someone who really cares
He waits for you to speak
He will answer all your prayers
* * *

GOOD NEWS IN A BAD WORLD
I heard the news from Africa
Another famine on the way.
A bomb goes off in Lancashire
It seems to happen every day.
Tragedy around us
Fear on every face
Headlines talk of misery
Bad news for the whole human race.
Good news in a bad world
We haven't been left alone
If we will reach out to him
He'll come and take us home.
* * *

FEARS
Petrified, I dare not stir
In case there's something in the air
I'm not moving out of bed
Duvet wrapped around my head
Shadows move across the floor
Is there someone at the door?
Bees, dogs, dark and mice
Everything that isn't nice
Fears surround us every day
But when You're here
They flee away.

LIVING ON THE EDGE

You say that it's all nonsense
That it won't come true
That I should live for today
And be like you
Why take the hard road
When compromise costs less
Forget about tomorrow
Today can hold success
But I'm living on the edge
Holding fast to what is true
It may be hazy now
But the light will break through

* * *

DON'T JUST SIT THERE

Don't just sit there
And watch the world die
Don't ignore the tears
While millions cry
You can make a difference
Bring life to this place
Wipe away the misery
Put a smile on someone's face
So don't just sit there
With idle hands
Jesus calls us into action
To fulfil His plans

* * *

I CAN'T KEEP IT IN

I cant keep it in
Got to let it out
I don't mind whispering
But I'd rather shout
I've found a secret
That's changed my life
He ended my sorrow
He stilled my strife
And I know He loves me
No matter how I feel
When I'm hurting
I know He can heal
You might think I'm wrong
Say it's a sin
But I've got to speak of Jesus
I just can't keep it in.

TAKE MY PEACE

Peace I give you
Take it to the world
Let them know my love
Like a banner unfurled
Tell them there's a better way
Where battles can cease
Tell them I have risen
Take my peace

* * *

BODY LANGUAGE

You turn away and hide your face
Questioning my role in the human race
Limbs that are twisted, head never still
No sign of intellect, mind or will
You interpret the signs and put me
                in a box
But I'm breaking out of your
                human locks
The messages are there, but in a
                different key
It's not in my appearance that
                You'll find the
Real me

* * *

ANGELS

We hear the sound of laughter
There is singing in the air
Our hearts are warmed with gladness
For angels are very near
But some of them are broken
With wings that cannot fly
And tears stream down their faces
Which also makes us cry
But angels are a gift from God
So let us stop the pain
Mend their broken hearts
And let them fly again

* * *

HANDS OF LOVE

We see the face of tragedy
And taste bitter tears
Feel stinging pangs of remorse
And whisper intimate fears

Death is running riot
Despair cuts like a knife
We ask the unthinkable question
Is this the end of life?

But hands of love are reaching out
See the scars and pain
For He has been to hell and back
So we can live again
* * *

KING WITH DIRTY HANDS
He is not found in regal splendour
Wall to wall pictures
Trappings of gold and silver
But in alley ways
Shop entrances
Lying on pavements
He is not surrounded by attendants
But by fishermen
Tax collectors
Drop outs
And cripples
There is no Rolls
But a dirty floor with wood shavings
And hands that reach out and touch
The untouchable.
He has dirty hands
But the dirt is ours
And only His blood makes us clean.
* * *

RUNNING MAN
See my shadow on the wall
Hear my pounding feet
I just keep on running
For I don't want to meet
Meaning truth and love
And reality
I would rather chase a myth
Believing I am free

Listen to my footsteps
Catch me if you can
Faster than the speed of light
I am the running man

I hide from obligation
And shelter from belief
When I hear a fairy tale
I sigh with relief
But my time is running out
For I see a wall
There's nowhere left to flee to
And I hear Him call
* * *

LIFELINE
Hear the clock strike midnight
Everyone's gone home
Dreams crumble into ashes
And you are left alone

A distant siren wails
Another life in pain
Leaving the question
Can you live again

And in the lights of the city
You always feel fine
But in the shadows of the night
You cry for a life line

The wind blows round your feet
You'd like to shelter from the storm
Feel strong arms around you
And know there's no more harm

There's One who knows your heart
The anguish and the fear
He gave His life for you
If you will draw near
* * *

MYSELF IN YOU
I've tried living the good life
Worshipping the sun
Living for today
And running for the fun

My promotional prospects
Have always been high
And although I look happy
You can see it's just a lie

I go out with the in crowd
On a Saturday night
We have a few bevvies
And try not to fight

I have a comfortable home
And a beautiful wife
Two point four children
But I still don't know the meaning
of life

I thought I'd maximised my potential
And there was nothing left to do
But you shattered my illusion
And I have found myself in You.
* * *

IN YOUR HANDS
I didn't know the way
Was afraid of each new day
Tears in the darkness
I didn't understand
Then I heard your voice
Realised I had a choice
Now the day has broken
For I am in your hands

When the tears fall down
Every time I wear a frown
You touch my heart
And reveal Your plans.
I will trust in You
For I know Your love is true
Whatever happens to me
I am in Your hands.
* * *

EYES OF THE WORLD
The eyes of the world
Are fixed on the heavens tonight
Straining through darkness
Searching for the light
How long will it be
Until we can be free?
The eyes of the world
Are fixed on the heavens tonight

The eyes of the world
Are looking for the day
When peace will come
And war will flee away
Longing hearts cry out
Waiting for his shout
The eyes of the world
Are looking for the day

The eyes of the world
See the time is near
When joy will come
And there is no more fear
He will reign as King
And our hearts will sing
The eyes of the world
See the time is near

SINGING IN THE RAIN
The car has broken down
Telly's on the blink
Water overflowing
Something nasty in the sink.
The sun has gone on holiday
Nothing left to eat
Everything is falling down
I cannot move my feet.

But as long as You are there
I can face the pain
I'll keep on singing in the rain.

Life is full of problems
Rain instead of sun
Just like a line of buses
There will always be another one
But if you put your trust in Jesus
He will stay with you
And when the shadows come
He'll bring you through.
* * *

SNAP SHOTS
I see a picture
Of a child who has no voice
But no-one listens
And she doesn't have a choice
Armies battle
On the same old piece of ground
Children dying
And no-one hears their sound

Snap shots of tears of laughter
Every picture tells a story
And only he can give us vision
To bring about his peace and glory

In the alley
She tries to find a bed
A card board box
Is the cushion for her head
And some are starving
While food is thrown away
And tears are falling
From the one who shows the way
* * *

COAST TO COAST
Watch the trees go by
Feel that I could fly
Another destination tonight
Wind blows through my hair
But I do not care
For I know that what I'm doing is right

Going coast to coast
I don't mind the miles
Because you're reaching out
Turning tears to smiles

Sometimes it's hard
But you hold the card
And I want to do what you ask
Fill me with your power
For the coming hour
Only in your love can I fulfil the task
* * *

WIPE AWAY MY TEARS
It's been such a long day
And nothing has gone right
I feel the comfort of evening
But I dread the night

The problems around me
Seem to tower above
And I would be swallowed up
But for Your love

But when I feel Your arms around me
And You calm my fears
You surround me with Your presence
And wipe away my tears

I remember the old days
When I was so alone
Lost and fearful
And so far from my home

Then I heard Your voice
Calling out to me
And You took my anguish
And said 'Rest in Me'.
* * *

HOLD ON TO YOUR DREAM
So many voices
Giving you their view
There are different opinions
But which is true?

You're looking for guidance
A way to survive
Break out of the prison
Of nine to five

Where are the answers?
You want to scream
Don't get caught in the nightmare
Hold on to your dream

There is One who understands
The way you feel
He came to show us
What is real

You don't have to settle
For second best
Give Him your life
He will do the rest.
* * *

RUNNING IN THE LIGHT

Shadows are falling across the moon
Could be the end of everything soon
So much destruction in the air
Is anyone listening and do they care?

War and pollution, death and hate
How did we get in such a state?
People are dying before our eyes
And we sit back and listen to lies.

Don't stand in the shadows
Or be afraid of the night
The darkness is fading
We're running in the light.

You're waiting for the break of day
When all sorrow will flee away
The earth will sing a brand new song
Don't drop your pace it won't be long

* * *

INVISIBLE DANCER

You look in my eyes
And see the hope
Wonder to yourself
How does he cope?

Words of consolation
You give to me
But although you're looking
You don't see

For I am an invisible dancer
Even though I can't leave my seat
But one day
I'll fly away
When I find my feet

I feel your pity
But I don't understand
I try to explain
It's in His hands

The chains are broken
That were holding me
And I dance in His presence
For I am free!

* * *

HOME

Home is where your heart is
A place to rest
A shelter from the storm
In the midst of the test

A place of belonging
Where I am free
Where the cares of the world
No longer hold me

I rest in your presence
For You have said 'Come
The door is open
And I am home'.

Chapter 12
Dance of Life (1995)

Alyn says: Escaping these shores we experience eastern Europe and west, travelling by sea, air and road. Working with friends brings much pleasure.

Introduction

Alyn Haskey is an extraordinary man. If you've ever met him, or seen him in action, you'll know exactly what I mean.

Many of us suspect that poets are really foppish men with handkerchiefs and billowing sleeves, who spend their days prancing around and composing odes to daffodils. Alyn certainly puts the lie to this. I have seen audiences deeply moved by his poetry readings. Ordinary men and women relate to what he says. People whose only real exposure to poetry was being forced to read Iambic Pentameters (whatever those might be) at school, and who never imagined that they could ever actually like a poem, find themselves enjoying his work.

And not merely enjoying it, but also being challenged by it. Through both his poetry and his person. Alyn constantly challenges our perceptions. We like to think of disabled people, for instance, as victims: recipients. We are not used to thinking of them as preachers and teachers: givers. We expect faith to be a log to cling to in the midst of the rapids, but Alyn shows it to be an oar to paddle back upstream. We instinctively look for power in strength, yet Alyn reaches into his own weakness - a weakness with which all of us can identity - to produce a power all of its own, capable of moving us to tears and, more importantly to change.

In this new volume of his poetry, Alyn once again challenges our perceptions. I feel honoured to have been asked to introduce these poems to you. You don't need qualifications to read them. You don't even need to like poetry. But, be warned: they are not for the faint-hearted.   Steve Chalke, Oasis Trust

STAIRWAY

I'm climbing the stairway to heaven
Hoping they will open the door
But with every step that I take
The nearer I am to the floor
I think that I've led a good life
And tried not to hurt anyone
Yet all my efforts seem useless
And my plans seem to come undone
I see a hand reach towards me
It is covered with scars and shame
Yet it holds out a crown of glory
And the writing declares my name
So I'm climbing the stairway to heaven
Confident that I will get in
For He has paid for my entry
When He died to cleanse me from my sin

WAITING

A clock ticks slowly
The sun has gone to sleep
Drops of icy water
As the season begins to weep
Memories are fading
Like an old photograph
And heavy feelings dominate
It's hard to raise a laugh
And waiting is so difficult
We almost want to bust
But He will never fail us
So let's obey and trust
* * *

POMP AND CIRCUMSPECTION

Land of Soaps and Tories
Dole queues on the rise
Homelessness around us
Death before our eyes
Broken promises ring out
Green shoots are in sight
Only true repentance
Will bring us into light
Turn to God in weakness
He will put it right.
* * *

JIGSAW

I've sussed out Father Christmas
And I know he isn't true
You can't rely on Batman
Or call in Doctor Who
So I will put my trust
In music, fashion and romance
Living for the moment
For you only get one chance
But when I see a sun rise
Or walk out in the rain
When hope comes out of tragedy
It makes me think again
I have put in all the pieces
Of my life's jigsaw
But the focal point is missing
Could it be there is something more?

SUNRISE

Shadows give way to light
As day overcomes the night
Dreams are chased from sight
Nightmares hide in fright
For day has come
As the night dies
He leads us on
Into the sunrise
* * *

CROSSING THE BORDER

The tension is rising
Search lights are on
A trigger happy hand
And we could be gone
Head full of doubt
Why are we here
Holding our breath
Tasting the fear
Crossing the border
At your command
Only your power
Gives us courage to stand
* * *

EYES ON THE PRIZE

Keep your eyes on the prize
And don't be pulled away
Don't be a late runner
Start from today
There's a race to be run
Before many eyes
So put on your shoes
And run for the prize
* * *

IN THE SAME BOAT

The wind is blowing
The tide is high
We seem to be sinking
And no-one hears us cry
The storm is raging
The battle is long

It's not my fault
It is him that's wrong
Don't point the finger
For we're in the same boat
If we all work together
We will keep afloat
* * *

GOLD
Of all the treasure I have found
Nothing compares to your sweet
sound
You call me out
From night to day
Dried my tears
Chased shadows away
And now I live
In your gentle hold
You are more precious
Than the finest gold
* * *

PARTY ANIMAL
I've got my invitation
And I won't be late
I'm going to a party
That will be great
The fun is never ending
And the music is out of sight
We will still be swinging
In the morning light
The party is forever
And entrance is free
For Jesus requests the pleasure
Of our company
* * *

DARE TO DREAM
Dare to dream
And not lose heart
Hold on to your hope
When life falls apart
Don't listen to doubt
Or sad old stories
God has a purpose

And it will end in glory
Give him your life
And see what he can do
Dare to dream in Jesus
For He makes them come true
* * *

THEY DON'T DO THAT THERE DO THEY?
They don't do that there do they?
I mean they're not the same
To see them out in public
It does seem such a shame
I thought they stayed in the houses
Locked behind iron gates
But I see them all around me
And they want to be my mates
They don't do that there do they?
I am quite surprised
Perhaps I ought to seek the truth
And not be fooled by lies
* * *

DANCING IN THE DARK
You can hear the music playing
Swaying to the beat
Caught in the shadow
Happy tapping feet
You do not hear the warning
For the rhythm drives you on
Danger all around you
And the world could soon be gone
You just keep on bopping
And think it's just a lark
You are running from the light
Dancing in the dark
* * *

THE FIRST TIME
The first time I met you
My heart began to sing
You touched my deepest hurts
And gave my spirit wings
The sunshine of your love
Has chased away the rain

The warmth of your healing
Has eased the bitter pain
The first time I met you
You whispered Come To Me
You fill me with your love
And you set me free
* * *

OUT OF THE DARKNESS
Out of the darkness you called me
Taking the scales from my eyes
Speaking truth into my heart
And banishing all the lies
Making me feel valued
Showing me how to be free
Once I was fearful of shadows
Now I am able to see
* * *

GOING THROUGH
THE MOTIONS
I'm showing a heart of compassion
Fighting for justice and peace
Trying to live an upright life
Hoping that war will cease
Making sure that my good side
Is always open to view
Hiding the doubts and weakness
And the feelings which are true
We are all going through the motions
Fingers crossed that no-one will see
All the pain and confusion
That is the real me
* * *

EXIT
Vibrations shaking heavy loads
Rumbles sound on distant roads
Glaring headlights pierce the sky
And I am left to wonder why
Silence reigns where laughter rang
No more tunes where music sang
Just an empty piece of ground
The night the circus left the town

GIFT OF LIFE
A gift of life is given
A treasure for us to share
A precious offering to the Lord
Which we must bless and care
We welcome you into our midst
May joy be in your heart
Let God's love fill you richly
As His spirit he imparts
* * *

UNTIL I COME HOME
I'm counting the miles
The tears and the smiles
As the days go rushing by
There's a hope in my heart
For I'm playing a part
In a plan that comes from on high

Sometimes it is tough
But you give me enough
To see that the task is done
And although I feel tired
By your power I'm inspired
As clouds give way to the sun

There are times on this journey
When I feel all alone
But I know that you are waiting
Until I come home
* * *

NOTHING SWEETER
There's nothing sweeter
Than a Happy Eater
Morning noon and night
With so much fudge
I cannot budge
My trousers feel too tight

Cream and tea
Hot coffee
Sandwiches cut real thick
Now I know
Why he has a glow
And looks as if he's being sick

CHOCOLATE BOX

A chocolate box and a thank-you card
An offering for working hard
It may not seem like much to you
But come and take a closer view
See those who have received new hope
An inner strength to help them cope
Blinded eyes that now can see
There is a way of being free
Tears of joy from those who cried
When His love touched them
                    deep inside
It might seem nothing at first sight
But I have felt His smile tonight
                    * * *

HOLDING ON

The pale sun of winter
Watery clouds of grey
An icy blast of wind
Heralds another day
And sometimes it's so easy
Answers come one by one
But even in the hard times
I'll be holding on
                    * * *

OPEN YOUR HEART

I can see in your eyes
The doubt and surprise
Making you think again
A smile on my face
I am part of the race
As we battle with the same pain

Just part of God's plan
I am no Superman
Willing to lend a hand
There's a place for us all
If we answer His call
And see what He has planned

All my chains are broken
I am ready to play my part
What will you do
He is calling to you
Open your heart

FEBRUARY BLUES

February blues
Worn out shoes
Waiting for some good news
Feeling tired
Not inspired
Like a boiler not yet fired
Frozen by the winter cold
My eyes are fixed on
Better gold
                    * * *

MUGGED

As I set out on my journey
I was mugged one day
I did not see it coming
And the thief got clean away
But just as I was coming round
Coping with my pain
A crowd of people passed me by
And I was mugged again

They don't see my humanity
But only stop and stare
Ignoring my potential
A suitable case for care
But then a stranger stopped
And took me by the hand
He healed my aching heart
Gave me strength to stand
                    * * *

SOS

Streets are full of faded dreams
City feels so cold
What happened to the rainbow
Where are the pots of gold

Hope has vanished like the wind
Sweet taste turns to sour
And with every step I take
Sense it's my last hour

Fear sits on my shoulder
Wrestling with doubt
But before the final bell
You will hear me shout

I'm sending out an S O S
Don't want to lose the fight
I've got my back against the ropes
Will someone save me tonight
* * *

STANDPOINT
Will you run
Or stand and fight
Encourage the darkness
Or spread the light
Choose today
Where you will go
Wave a white flag
Or face the foe
The time has come
To make a stand
And bring back
Glory to this land
* * *

IN FOR A GRILLING
In for a grilling
Save a pound
Flaming whoppers
All around
Excited eyes
Of girls and boys
Burger coke
Cakes and toys
Lovers stare
Making plans
Relish dripping
From their hands
Sixty per cent more
Is their claim
Strange how it always
Tastes the same
* * *

JUST ANOTHER DAY?
The sun has risen
A blazing sky
Shards of light
Catch the eye

Freshness springs
From fields of green
Untold glories
Yet to be seen
And I'm awake
And on my way
Glad to be alive
On this day
* * *

SANCTUARY
Running from the gates of hell
Will we survive who can tell
Peace like a dream fades away
Diminished by the light of day
A place to hide is what we seek
Where we can feel both frail and weak
A haven of truth where we can tarry
Safe within His sanctuary
* * *

THINK OF A NUMBER
Think of a number
Four plus two
Make your selection
It could be you
A roll of the dice
Watch the ball spin
Great anticipation
Will you win
Think of a number
How about one
For only with Him
Can life be won
* * *

A FOREIGN SHORE
On a foreign shore
In another land
My head is full of doubts
Is this what you planned
Taxing conversations
The questions are not clear
Wondering to myself
What am I doing here

But you've brought me to this place
To fulfil your call
For your love has no frontiers
It reaches out to all
* * *

ON THE LINE

The world is closing in
There's nowhere left to run
Darkness presses downwards
Clouds conceal the sun

Enemies on every side
My heart is full of fear
What happened to the good times
Why don't I feel you near

Yet though the storm clouds gather
The outcome will be fine
For when I call your name
I know you're on the line
* * *

SILENT PARTNER

We sit across the table
Your smile speaks welcome
Busy conversations
Take place all around
About the weather
The state of the nation
The music
Plans for the future
Words fly back and forth
But you never speak to me
* * *

WASTE LAND

Pitted holes
On the ground
Shattered dreams
Lie around
Desolation on every side
Images of life
Which have died
But the days of the locust
Have run their race
And life springs up
By His grace

THE SAME OLD WAR SONGS

Don't sing the same old war songs
Pretending you long for peace
Selling weapons of destruction
And wondering why the killing won't cease
Ignoring the coverage on telly
Hoping it will go away
While you build your commercial empire
And get richer by the day
So don't sing the same old war songs
For we're all getting quite tired
And there's one who will change the music
And you'll find it's you who is fired.
* * *

LOVE IS THE POWER

Love is the power that changes hearts
It reaches into the deepest parts
Brings a new vision
And gives us fresh sights
Is not fearful of darkness
But shines in the light
Love is the power
He speaks by His breath
His love is forgiveness
That conquers death

ONE DAY I'M GOING
TO DANCE

One day I'm going to dance
I will tap with my feet
And will move gracefully
The music will lift me
I will spin like a top
And cut the air
I will skip to the tune
Flow with the beat
And my dance will go on forever
You may question
But I tell you
One day I'm going to dance
* * *

MAZE

Going round in circles
My head is full of doubt
So easy to get in here
Can't find my way out
Arrows pointing everywhere
But everything looks the same
It seemed a good idea
Now I don't know why I came
Longing for a voice
To show me the way
Lead me on to safety
Can't you hear me pray
* * *

ISLANDS

From shore to shore
Across the land
The day has dawned
As it was planned
People rise
To face the day
The race has started
We are now away
Though sometimes storms
Crash the shoreline
In spite of doubt
It will be fine
For though we seem lost on the sea
Separated and not free
The King will come
Again to reign
And we shall be one
Once again

MOVING

Two steps forward
Jump to the side
Clap your hands
Take a ride
Moving

Feel the rhythm
Sense the beat
Heart is pounding
Tap my feet
Moving

The music is good
Song is sweet
You touched my heart
Turned on the heat
I'm moving

ETERNALLY YOURS

Like a puppet without a string
I was lifeless on the ground
Looking for a treasure
That would never be found
Then I heard your voice calling to me
And you picked me up
And helped me to see
That you are the answer
From you all love pours
I am alone no longer
Eternally yours

Chapter 13
Band aid For a Broken World (1997)

Alyn says: Things are sent to try us, and hopes are sometimes pushed aside, but they don't die. Enforced rest may be frustrating but in God we trust and He will put it right.

Editor's note: These are a selection of the poems that will be published later in 1997.

GIVE ME SOMETHING FOR THE PAIN
Give me something for the pain
When I think it hurts my brain
Can somebody tell me why
Many weep and others die
Why do dreams fade to dust
All that glitters shows signs of rust
The questions are so hard to bear
Does anybody really care
So before I go insane
Give me something for the pain

* * *

DRAWING IN
Leaves are floating on the breeze
The year begins to take it's ease
Watery sun plays hide and seek
And blue skies run feeling meek
Summer's thread is wearing thin
See the nights are drawing in

* * *

DESPERATE
I believe in Santa Claus
And his jet-pack sleigh
He brings me all my presents
Every Christmas day

I hope there is a Santa Claus
Or else I will be sad
For he's the one who makes me good
Instead of being bad

Please let there be a Santa Claus
With clothes so red and bright
Someone to look out for
In the shadows of the night

But if there is no Santa Claus
Where shall I put my trust
Who will put my life together
When dreams have turned to dust

* * *

NOW
Break all the chains
Lighten the load
A time of home-coming
For those on the road
Establishing justice
For the poor and the lost
Giving back freely
Not counting the cost
Trusting in God
For the things that we need
No sowing or reaping
No planting of seed
Now is the time
For all to be free
Joining together
In great jubilee

* * *

FIRST DAY
Bells ring a song of joy
Mixed with hope and fear
Looking back in gladness
Welcoming another year
The days ahead look misty
Who can really tell
Whether they will be heaven
Or a descent into hell
He who has the answers
Will show us the way
For he is the signpost
For this first day

I'LL BE THERE FOR YOU
At the end of the day
When you are feeling tired
And it's all gone wrong
You are not inspired
The dreams take forever
To come to fruition
Nothing is happening
Where is the vision
Call out my name
And know that it's true
In the midst of the loneliness
I'll be there for you
* * *

PEACE IN THE STORM
The wind is blowing hard
Waves are flying high
Clouds are sprinting madly
Racing across the sky
Fear on every face
Our hands upon our heart
Hoping against the odds
We won't be torn apart
But there is one who loves us
In him there is no harm
He is there beside us
Giving peace in the storm
* * *

FIRST LIGHT
Shadows linger in the darkness
Fearful of the dawn
Clinging fast to the night
Holding back the morn
Suddenly an earthquake
Breaks with all it's might
Death gives way to life
And we see the first light
* * *

LOADS OF MONEY
I am going to town this morning
To see what I can buy
I haven't shopped for a week
If I don't go I will die
I don't know what I'm after
But it doesn't really matter
As long as I take out my purse
And see some money scatter
It could be a car
A drink at the bar
Or a holiday in the sun
And I'll push back the fears
That ring in my ears
Saying is it really fun
* * *

PERCEPTION
They have seen me
And think they are experts
They do not credit me
                with intelligence
But treat me like a baby
They do not provide facilities
For I am not expected to do
                anything worthwhile
Instead they keep me where it's safe
Provide just enough to meet my needs
And to satisfy decency
Wherever I go there are barriers
For I am tolerated
But not accepted for who I am
* * *

SUNSHINE
Sunshine streams into my room
Brightness scatters night and gloom
Music draws me on to dance
Knowing I am not here by chance
Out I go to meet the day
See what treasures come my way
Through blue or grey it will be fine
In the warmth of his sunshine
* * *

A LAND OF PLENTY

A place to rest
And take our ease
An end to fighting
A lasting peace
Good things abound
On every hand
Milk and honey
A promised land
But the hungry cry
For lack of food
The media bring us
Bad not good
Many sit
With idle hands
Poverty and injustice
Stalk the land
Yet he waits
With patient heart
And when we turn
The dream will start
* * *

LIVE AGAIN

In the valley
Dark and bare
Where death reigns
I stand and stare
Ruin of ages
Lies around
Like dry bones
On dusty ground
Then a voice
Like refreshing rain
Speaks his word
Live again
* * *

LEAVES

Leaves turn from green to brown
And with the wind come crashing down
Sings of decay obscure the ground
New shoots are so rarely found
Though now it is a desolate scene
In hope we wait to see new green

PRICELESS

When you look in the mirror
What do you see
The face of a loser
With no guarantee
A faceless statistic
With no value at all
No one will care
Whether you fall
But wait just a minute
It's not such a mess
There is one who lives you
To Him you're priceless
* * *

REJOICE

When heartache cuts like a knife
Every action threatens life
Frustration stands in my way
Spoiling yet another day
In darkness comes a gentle voice
Then I remember and rejoice
* * *

WHISPERS

A gentle breeze
Sways in the trees
Words I cannot hear
A silent wind
Speaks to me
Take heart in your fear
When skies are grey
Or on golden day
Know that I am near
* * *